Protestant Churches and Reform Today

Lawrence L. Durgin
Daisuke Kitagawa
William H. Lazareth
J. Lynn Leavenworth
Lewis S. Mudge
Daniel J. O'Hanlon, S.J.
Colin W. Williams

William J. Wolf, *Editor*

 The Seabury Press • New York

ACKNOWLEDGMENTS

Grateful acknowledgment is given to the following authors and publishers for permission to reprint copyrighted material:

Christian Century—Harold E. Fey, editorial, October 23, 1940. Copyright 1940 Christian Century Foundation.

Fortress Press—Luther D. Reed, *The Lutheran Liturgy*

Judson Press—Norman H. Maring and Winthrop S. Hudson, *A Baptist Manual of Polity and Practice*

LCA Board of Social Ministry—*Church and State—A Lutheran Perspective*

LCA Board of Theological Education—Conrad Bergendoff, *The Lutheran Church in America*

The Lutheran Companion—Conrad Bergendoff, "The Meaning of Lutheran Unity," November 5, 1952

The Newman Press—Michael J. Taylor, *The Protestant Liturgical Renewal*

Sheed & Ward—Hans Küng, *The Council in Action*

University of Chicago Press—Winthrop Hudson, *American Protestantism*

Contents

Introduction by the Editor   1

1.   Toward an Ecumenical Theology
      of Mission and Ministry   8
            by Daisuke Kitagawa

2.   Do the Baptists Have Treasures?   24
            by J. Lynn Leavenworth

3.   Christ Has Set Us Free   46
            by Lawrence L. Durgin

4.   The Future of American Lutheranism   71
            by William H. Lazareth

5.   On Being Free for Christ's Work in
      the World   100
            by Colin W. Williams

6.   Can Presbyterians Be Reformed?   124
            by Lewis S. Mudge

Epilogue   143
            by Daniel J. O'Hanlon, S.J.

Contributors' Notes   151

Introduction

The Second Vatican Council has shattered once for all any illusion that reform was the special preserve of Protestants. Not only has it done this; it has also challenged the non-Roman churches to ask whether they may still justly consider themselves as Reformed churches. Had this development been prophesied only five years ago, it could have been dismissed as avant-garde speculation. Now it is solid fact, reversing a situation some four hundred years old in the West.

For a long time it seemed that the word "reform" was suspect in Roman Catholicism, because of its association with the Protestant Reformation. It was. It is not suspect any longer, save possibly in some extremely conservative curial circles. The theological work of Karl Rahner, Ives Congar, and Hans Küng has been confirmed by the actions of the Council. These men are no longer lonely prophetic figures, but representative Catholic spokesmen for the theology of the Roman Catholic Church today and in the future.

They have quite disarmed the suspicions of non–Roman Catholics by the power and realism of their criticism of their own church, while yet remaining profoundly loyal to it. The captious professional anti-Catholic will find, time and again, his criticisms applied even more thoroughly to the church by them and by many of the Council fathers. No non-Roman Christian can possibly doubt in the face of such openness, such undefensive admission, such piercing critique, that the Holy Spirit is at work renewing the church.

Pope John XXIII pioneered in calling the Council, and Pope Paul VI continues in the same spirit, bringing to the task gifts of clear analysis and executive responsibility. In his opening allocution Pope Paul defined four purposes for the Council: "the understanding of the Church, its reform (*renovatio*), the recovery of unity between all Christians, and the dialogue of the Church with contemporary men." The preamble to the Constitution on the Sacred Liturgy, promulgated in December of 1963, officially commits the Roman Catholic Church to reform:

This sacred Council has several aims in view: it desires to impart an ever increasing vigor to the Christian life of the faithful; to adapt more suitably to the needs of our own times those institutions which are subject to change; to foster whatever can promote union among all who believe in Christ; to strengthen whatever can help to call the whole of mankind into the household of the Church. The Council therefore sees particularly cogent reasons for undertaking the reform and promotion of the liturgy.

It was the failure of the medieval church to reform itself "in head and members" which necessitated the Protestant Reformation. The Counter-Reformation actually accomplished a very considerable reform within the Roman Church, much more than Protestants in the age of polemics would admit, but the Council of Trent unfortunately did its work with a view toward polemics and victory for itself. What is plainly taking place before our eyes today is continued reformation with a view toward reconciliation in a genuinely ecumenical spirit. Bishop Angus Dun has described this remarkable development:

What looked to many of us outside as an ecclesiastical fortress, bent on guarding its ancient treasures, begins to show itself as a great household of faith and charity, eager to establish brotherly relationships, to understand and to be understood. All this could hardly have happened so quickly if there had not been within the whole Catholic community many bishops, priests, and theologians eager to come out and make contact. The Pope has released what was waiting to be released.[1]

Hans Küng has been the most articulate spokesman for reform. Gladly embracing the Latin formula *ecclesia semper reformanda* ("the church always needing to be reformed") which characterized the Calvinist reform, he urges the Council to meet the real problems posed by other Christians. His triumphal speaking tour to the United States after the first session of the Council helped American Catholics to express their own developing commitment toward reform. *The Council and Reunion*, published in 1961, acted like a catalyst on Roman Catholic world opinion just before the Council. *The Council in Action*, published after the first session and composed in large measure of his lectures before groups of bishops in Rome, was a powerful instrument in converting many to ecumenism and reform.

The only way for the Ecumenical Council to make an essential contribution towards preparing for reunion is through a renewal of the Catholic Church by carrying out the justified demands of the other side in the light of the Gospel of Jesus Christ; a renewal of the Catholic Church, springing, indeed, from her own essential nature as it has always been, but at the same time—this is the decisive thing—*fulfilling the justified demands of Lutherans, Calvinists, Orthodox, Anglicans, and Free Churchmen in the light of the Gospel of Jesus Christ*. Let it be the Gospel of Christ which decides, as between other Christians and ourselves, which of their demands are justified and which are not.[2]

Even if the Roman Catholic Church had not embraced reform, it would be imperative for the Protestant churches to continue the process of reformation, for the simple reason that a "reformed" church which ceases to allow itself to be constantly reformed is a contradiction in terms. "A reformation which stops is not a reformation."

A great deal of Protestant energy has been channeled into criticism of the "proud" claim to infallibility by the Roman Catholic Church. There are extremely serious issues here arising from the definitions of the First Vatican Council, but perhaps some attention to the beam in our own eyes is imperative now. The very title of a "Reformed Church" is suspect of either ecclesiastical pride or the absolutizing of a special tradition. *Ecclesia reformata* always needs to be modified by *ecclesia semper reformanda* ("a reformed church always open to the need to be reformed").

Would it not be a strange paradox in history if the Roman Catholic Church carried through so thorough a reformation that it left behind the Protestant churches, should they continue to speak the slogans of the sixteenth century but refuse to face the conditions of the world or of the Roman Church in the twentieth century? Karl Barth can hardly be accused of "catholicizing," for he has written his vast dogmatics in conscious opposition again and again to what he understands to be the Catholic position. Yet even he begins to sound a warning:

How would things look if Rome (without ceasing to be Rome) were one day simply to overtake us and place us in the shadows, so far as the renewing of the Church through the Word and the Spirit of the Gospel is concerned? What if we should discover that the last are first and the first last, that the voice of the Good Shepherd should find a clearer echo over there than among us? [3]

The Protestant churches of course have been facing the tasks of reform for a long time on a number of levels. Prophetic voices have been criticizing the suburban captivity of Protestantism, its weakness in the inner city, its outdated and outmoded agrarian and bourgeois climate. The theme of

Church-in-the-world has been dramatized by centers and groups dedicated to renewal. One whole wing of the Ecumenical Movement has emphasized the atrophied sense of mission. Individuals have been urging the church to speak a meaningful message to the modern world by improving its "communication," by "demythologizing" its message, by advocating a "religionless Christianity" for a "secular world come of age."

In spite of all this sound and fury, however, it must seriously be asked how much of this program of reform has really penetrated to the center of Protestantism. The Roman Catholic Church demonstrates its seriousness on the issue by engaging in an Ecumenical Council. What would be the equivalent on the Protestant side? Should each denomination call a council to commit its membership responsibly to reform? Are the ten-day or two-week ecumenical meetings like Faith and Order in Montreal in 1963 any longer adequate to the task, especially since this type of council has no real authority for its constituent churches? Is there too little sustained and constructive talk in Protestantism and too much destructive whipping of the churches by individuals eager to exploit? Or is there too much Protestant discussion and too little official Protestant action?

Even if all were well with us in heeding what the Spirit is saying to the churches in our kind of world, and even if we were growing together through our participation in the Ecumenical Movement to the point that our dividedness as churches was beginning to yield to the grace of union, there would still remain the specific challenge of Roman Catholic reform. What does this historical fact mean for us today?

Let us allow Hans Küng, who has so courageously challenged his own communion, to speak to us about our responsibility:

We have described the task set for us Catholics as reunion through carrying out the justified demands of Protestants in the light of the Gospel of Jesus Christ. The corresponding program for Protestants needs to be stated as clearly: reunion through carrying out the justified demands of *Catholics* in the light of that same Gospel of Jesus Christ. We Catholics, too, have demands, and big demands, to make of the Protestant churches. A reformation that stops is not a reformation. The adjective "reformed" as applied to a church (whether in a Lutheran or Calvinist sense) must not be a pretext for a timid rejection of new reforms. As Schleiermacher said, "The Reformation is still going on." It does not absolutely have to go on in the direction of Schleiermacher. Why should it be impossible for such reform sometimes to turn in the direction of the Catholic Church?—not in the sense of cheap external catholicizing and imitation, but in the sense of a re-examination of one's own position and one's own protests in the light of the Gospel of Jesus Christ; in the sense of honest self-examination and courageous, energetic measures of self-improvement. There is in the Scriptures—or so it seems to us Catholics, and many Protestant theologians, not catholicizers, agree with us—so much that is not attended to enough or understood enough or taken seriously enough in the Protestant churches. We rejoice over everything that has happened during the last few decades in the Protestant churches towards the fulfillment of what is valid in Catholic demands; we think particularly of the renewal of theology, of liturgy, and of the idea of the Church. We have taken innumerable steps towards each other, but there are innumerable steps still to take, from both sides.[4]

This book addresses itself to the question of Reform today in the Protestant Churches. The contributors are respected young theologians in their churches, and their essays articulate in an unofficial but representative way the problems of reform that are so urgently felt by churchmen, particularly younger churchmen. Each contributor speaks from his own tradition: Anglican (Episcopalian), Baptist, United

Church of Christ, Lutheran, Methodist, and Presbyterian in that order. And each has sought with openness to respond to Father Küng's invitation.

The book also carries an Epilogue by the Rev. Daniel J. O'Hanlon, S.J., who was invited to comment from his point of view on these essays. Although he speaks frankly, indeed sharply, that the essays, for the most part, do not respond to legitimate Catholic demands, Father O'Hanlon, nonetheless, points to significant concerns that the contributors discuss, which Roman Catholics also share. The important contribution which Father O'Hanlon makes here is to call attention sharply to those theological questions beyond mission that need to be discussed in the ecumenical framework. In doing this, he contributes to this symposium a balance that is most welcome and carries forward the developing dialogue.

The spirit of this joint enterprise might be expressed in the words of the Central Committee of the World Council of Churches, in its statement on the Vatican Council.

Renewal in one church is a source both of encouragement and of challenge to all other churches. The Central Committee invites the member churches to continue to pray both that, through the further labors of the Vatican Council, the power and grace of the Holy Spirit may be given to the Roman Catholic Church for the renewal of its life and also that, by the same Spirit, all churches may be quickened and renewed.[5]

WILLIAM J. WOLF

1

Daisuke Kitagawa:

Toward an Ecumenical Theology of Mission and Ministry

The Protestant Reformation of the sixteenth century was, in perspective, a *reform*-ation movement from within the Church, while the contemporary Ecumenical Reformation, if I may be permitted to use the phrase here, is more of a movement toward a re-*formation* of the Church under the pressure of the world—the secular world, the world-in-history. The desired re-formation, however, cannot be realized apart from a thoroughgoing renewal of the Church, even in her divided state. Such a renewal, furthermore, is possible only when the Church, under the guidance of the Holy Spirit, honestly confronts the world and re-examines what her mission in and to that world is. This being my basic premise, I shall dwell, in this paper, more upon the world than on the Church.

There is a profound sense in which the contemporary renewal of the Church is a result of the Church's rediscovery of the world, not only as God's own creation but, even more importantly, as the locus of God's action in history, and concomitant with this is the discovery of her own mission to the world. At long last a substantial number of Christian theologians, representative of the major confessional groupings, are now taking seriously what Frederick Denison Maurice emphasized just about a century ago and what Eastern Orthodox theology has always been based upon, namely, the theological tenet that the world has once and forever been redeemed by Christ. What makes the second half of the twentieth century so significant in church history is the fact that this theological truth has been increasingly recognized as an empirical truth by many Christians. Without this recognition neither the Ecumenical Movement, as we know it, would have been possible, nor Vatican Council II, nor the profound appreciation of that Council by both Orthodox and Protestant communions.

Legacy of the Missionary Movement

The Church rediscovered the world in the terms in which we have been speaking chiefly through the "foreign" missionary movement. This rediscovery came after the Counter-Reformation on the part of the Roman Church, and chiefly in the nineteenth century on the part of Western Protestantism. It is important to our discussion here that we examine these two developments together.

While the Protestant Reformers were preoccupied with purging the Church from within, the dynamics of the Counter-Reformation pushed the renewed Roman Church into the world of heathenism, as if, humanly speaking, to make up for the loss within Christendom by a gain from the outside. This thrust was spearheaded by the Society of Jesus; the Franciscans, Dominicans, and a host of missionary orders soon followed. Though the missionary movement of the Roman Church was inseparably linked with the maritime imperialism of the Iberian Empire, and therefore an element of territorial aggrandisement was admittedly prominent in it, it opened the eyes of the Church to parts of the world till then unknown to her, great continents inhabited by millions of souls for whom Christ had died.

After the Reformation, the historic schism of the Western Church, the Protestant churches continued to be preoccupied with matters of purity of doctrine, liturgy, and church polity in the light of the sole criterion of the Scripture. With their emphasis on "the priesthood of all believers," the Protestant churches inevitably came to be concerned almost exclusively with the individual and his interior life. This led to the rise of continental Pietism and English Puritanism, movements which in turn gave birth to the Protestant foreign missionary movement of the eighteenth and, especially, of the nineteenth centuries.

One must not forget that William Cary, commonly acclaimed as the founder of the modern missionary movement, was moved by the heroic missionary efforts which had been made by the continental Pietists (e.g., the Royal Danish Mission to Tranquebar), who in their turn had been initially stimulated by the pioneering missionary effort of the Puritan divine John Eliot among the North American Indians of New England. When this foreign missionary work became organized, first in Britain and then in North America, it was done as an interconfessional undertaking—the London Missionary Society, the American Board of Commissioners for Foreign Missions. The host of confessionally oriented missionary societies which followed overshadowed the basically interconfessional outreach of the initial foreign missionary movement, with the result that what one might call "confessional colonialism" became a conspicuous feature in Protestant missionary effort during the nineteenth century.

What distinguished Protestant mission from Roman Catholic mission, it may be fairly accurately said, was that Protestant mission addressed itself to the individual, and Roman Catholic mission to the community of people. Moreover, the Pietist/Puritan emphasis on the essential sinfulness of unredeemed humanity was not only of major importance to Protestant mission theology but also served the Protestant missionary as a means of relating himself to the not-yet-redeemed heathen. In fact, it was not necessary for him to know anything about a heathen people, save that they were sinners and their souls were doomed to perish unless they accepted the gospel of Christ.

Despite their differences in orientation to mission, both the Protestant and Roman Catholic churches, in the post-Reformation period, crossed the boundaries of Christendom and, in their respective ways, engaged the world. If the Roman Catholic mission was inseparably linked with the maritime imperialism of the Spanish-Portuguese Empire, the Protestant mission was inextricably linked with the colonial imperialism of the Western powers in the post-Industrial Revolution period. Thorough conversion of a heathen to Christianity was believed to involve the forsaking of his primitive way of life and adaptation to the missioner's civilized (i.e., Western) way of life! Indeed, Protestant mission meant *ipso facto* the expansion of Western industrial civilization.

Both Roman Catholic and Protestant Christians have thus been engaged with the *world* in deadly seriousness for a long period; but now, at last, both recognize the elemental fact that before any missionary stepped out of Christendom, the whole world—including those areas traditionally designated as "heathendom"—had already been visited by the risen Christ had been redeemed. Indeed, he stands in the midst of other peoples as their Saviour as much as ours. Therefore, the Church sends her sons and daughters to these other areas to point to her Master, who has always been at work in every part of the world among all peoples. Moreover, our cognizance of this fact is the foundation which God himself has laid for the contemporary movement of Ecumenical Reformation. For, in the face of this freshly revealed fact of God's world, how can the Church remain complacent about her own internal division? The Ecumenical Reformation, which is dawning today, is no less than a movement to restructure the Church, and while stemming from the renewal of her spirit in her still divided state, it points to her mission and apostolate in the world.

Issues Confronting the Church in the Contemporary World

The world rediscovered by the Church as the locus of God's action in history confronts the Church with a series of issues to which the Church, in order to be the Church, cannot remain indifferent. A few of the outstanding ones will be discussed here briefly.

INTEGRITY OF THE SECULAR.   First and foremost, the theological significance of the secular world itself needs to be more fully articulated. It is the basic premise of Judeo-Christian theology that the world in its totality is God's creation, and the so-called "secular" realm is just as much under God's reign as the "sacred," or "religious." God is not a "specialist in religion." Furthermore, the secular is not important in the eyes of God merely as an appendage to the sacred, but in its own right.

Theologically, the secular has its own integrity: first, as the context within which a man becomes a Christian and bears witness to the gospel, and the Church is the Church; and second, as the object of the redemptive work of God as much as of his creative work—thus a realm to which the Church has to address itself. For example, politics as a process of collective action of men in a pluralistic society is, ought to be, secular. Christian witness in reference to race relations, human misery of all sorts, fulfillment of the God-given potentialities of every child, or peace and social justice among nations is impossible apart from political action either as a process through which, or as a context in which, witness takes place. That a Christian chooses politics as his "Christian vocation" (i.e., chooses to be a professional politician) is not to "spiritualize" politics nor to mix religion and politics. It should mean that through his ethically responsible and professionally competent participation in politics, he makes politics serve the political needs of mankind—not religious needs or the needs of Christian people alone. And in that he addresses himself as a Christian to politics—an object of God's redemptive work—he witnesses to his Christian faith within the context of politics. In so doing, he upholds the integrity of politics as politics. Likewise, a Christian in education is a technically competent educator who makes education serve the needs of humanity, not the vested interest of professional educators as a group.

The same principle also applies to science, business, industry, intergroup relations, international relations, and so on. For a Christian to be engaged in any of these does not mean to "Christianize" them, but to be Christian within them both as contexts of his Christian witness and as objects of his Christian concern.

What Christian theology traditionally calls the "redemption of the world" ought now, therefore, to be redefined in terms of the integrity of the secular. Otherwise, the phrase will not mean much to modern man in a post-Christian culture. On the other hand, full acceptance and acknowledgment of the secular for what it really is will provide a common ground for all religious groups to engage in creative dialogue with one another; and it will contribute simultaneously to the renewal of the Church and the growth of ecumenical fellowship.[1]

TECHNOLOGY AND THE REVOLUTION IN THE ETHICS OF WORK.   For the first time in history, man finds himself capable both of annihilating the entire civilization and of re-creating human society throughout the world. Usually our age is discussed from a negative point of view: industrial automation or cybernation is talked about in terms of mass unemployment; technology, in terms of man being the machine's slave; nuclear power, in terms of the threat of total war; urbanization, in terms of the congestion and slums in large cities. Yet it is the positive aspects of the age which make it the most exciting in human history. Here, however, only a few questions of crucial importance from the ethical standpoint can be considered.

Man has traveled a long way to the technological civilization we know, starting from the primitive stage of food-gathering, in which he was completely dependent on nature and its caprices, then through various intermediate stages to the present stage of food-producing and food-manufacturing, in which he knows how to manipulate nature for his benefit. During this development man has had to toil to maintain his existence. "In the sweat of your face you shall eat bread till you return to the ground" (Gen. 3:19). Toil has been accepted as an integral part of human existence, and it has been sanctified as a virtue especially in Protestant ethics. Living has been turned into a sort of reward for toil. "If any one will not work, let him not eat" (2 Thess. 3:10). Thus the phrase "to make a living" is accepted as the chief motive of work. Honest living is assumed to be possible only through honorable industry, and industry *qua* industry is regarded as honorable, regardless of the meaningless drudgery or painful toil it may involve. To live as a self-respecting person, man has to engage in work; and this work has become synonymous with toiling and being paid a wage for the toil, so as to be able to buy one's own bread. With such an orientation man can hardly enjoy life, for enjoying life is only possible as a sort of *bonus* to which only those who have worked with diligence are entitled.*

Now technology is making it less and less necessary for man to toil and possible for him to enjoy life and its abundance. Is this ethically wrong? Is not technology also a gift of God? If so, then are we not required radically to reconsider the traditional ethics of work? This is basically a theological task, in which Christians of all traditions can and must participate. How should Genesis 3:19 and Second Thessalonians 3:10 be interpreted in the age of computing machines and automation? If we accept the sanctity of life itself, does it not follow that every child born into our society has the inalienable right to live, with or without employment? And as long as our society taken as a whole has more than enough resources to support everybody and then some to spare, do we not have the God-given responsibility to so organize, even restructure, our society as to enable every man, woman, and child to live lives free from want with respect to basic material needs? With modern technology and its product, cybernation, are we not entering a stage of human civilization in which work as a creative process is at last possible?

METROPOLIS AS A NEW CREATION.   Man has been building cities throughout history. "Cain knew his wife, and she conceived and bore Enoch; and he built a city, and called the

---

* I owe these insights to Robert Theobold, a professional economist whose published works include: *The Challenge of Abundance* (a Mentor paperback), *The Rich and the Poor* (a Mentor paperback).

name of the city after the name of his son Enoch" (Gen. 4:17). This biblical myth suggests that building a city is as natural to man as having a family. "Come, let us make bricks. . . . Come, let us build ourselves a city, and a tower with its top in the heavens. . . ." (Gen. 11:3-4). The legend of the Tower of Babel is the typical story of human civilization: man's effort to build a city whose tower reaches heaven—and his failure in this effort.

Yet the vision of the perfect city has always been part of man's outlook. The old Jerusalem was idealized by the Psalmist: "Jerusalem is built as a city that is at unity in itself" (Ps. 122:3, BCP). And in the New Testament we read: "Then I saw a new heaven and a new earth. . . . And I saw the holy city, new Jerusalem, coming down out of heaven from God" (Rev. 21:1-2).

Historically, however, while man has been the builder of his city, its growth and extension has been largely a matter of accident beyond his control. From marketing center and military fort, to transportation and industrial center, the city grew where nature, mostly in terms of geography, made it most convenient. Today these cities are failing to meet men's needs in many ways, and we hear much about the city and its problems. Yet today, thanks to modern technology, man can build a city pretty much according to his own specifications, even though they are not always perfect. The important thing is that his specifications can be followed, and that therefore he has the moral responsibility to make his specifications meet the *human* needs of those who are to dwell in this city. It is at this point that theology has the opportunity to make a substantive contribution toward city-planning.

Uncontrolled megalopolitan sprawl is no more desirable than leaving the blighted inner city uncleared, for both are harmful to the total well-being of man. All the technical skills to operate highly efficient machines to build a city will not build a city "at unity in itself" without planning that is theologically oriented. This is, in one sense at least, what is meant by man's participation in God's creation. The world —the *kosmos*—is locally embodied in the city or metropolis, and man is invited by the Lord of creation to share in the building of this new creation.

This is not to say that we are to build a "Christian" city, or even a city the government of which is in the hands of Christians. The city the Christians are to share in building will be a local embodiment of the secular world and, therefore, of secular society; and the Church must learn how to be the Church in it. This will require, it is deemed certain, a radical restructuring of the Church in its institutional aspect. What kind of administrative structure does the Christian community—always a minority in the world—need if it is to be the Church in the metropolis, "the light of the world and the salt of the earth"? This is a far more urgent question than whether historic episcopate in the chain of apostolic succession is essential for the sacrament celebrated to be truly a sacrament. For the question of how the Church can best participate in the building of the city is the very substance of the question how the Church is to be the Church today in urban culture.[2] This question can be dealt with adequately only in the forum of ecumenical conversation.

For those in the Anglican tradition, as well as those in the Roman Catholic and Eastern Orthodox, this question leads to a radical re-examination of the traditional parish as a geographically defined area within the boundaries of which all souls belong to its cure. For this traditional concept of the parish is no longer tenable anywhere in the world, including England, where both secularism and religious (or ecclesiastical) pluralism prevail. The same applies to certain parts of Europe where the system of *Landeskirche* is still in effect, in principle at least. To raise this question is to open imme-

diately the subject of the mission and ministry of the Church
in today's world.

STATUS, ROLE, AND FUNCTION OF WOMEN.   Secularism,
technology, and cybernation all point to man's liberation
from the tyranny of nature.* As long as man was enslaved
to nature, the biologically rooted difference in the psycho-
somatic structures in men and women inevitably resulted in
their having different roles and functions in society. But with
man's increasing emancipation from nature, many of these
traditional distinctions have become theoretically untenable.
Evidence of this may be seen in the almost unlimited employment opportunities for technically qualified women in
every imaginable field, including the military services—practically the only exception being the sacred ministry in the
Roman Catholic, Eastern Orthodox, and Anglican traditions.

These changes in the roles and functions of women have
had, and will continue to have, far-reaching impact upon
family life, especially in the realm of parent-child relationships, and also upon the role and function of the family as
the basic human institution in society.

ETHNO-CULTURAL AND RACIAL GROUPS IN MASS SOCIETY.
Intellectually, one of the most difficult things to comprehend
about the modern age is the fact that racial problems continue
to remain acute all over the world, even among people who
are well-educated, and of high social standing and means.
One would expect these people to be completely free from
racial prejudices based on ignorance and unscientific myths,
and to be equally free from anxiety stemming from economic
insecurity. More disturbing, if not startling, is the fact that

* It is well to note in passing that "our secular society may be seen as
largely the product of the Christian West" (Munby), and that secularism
is a sign of the world "come of age," in the well-known words of Dietrich
Bonhoeffer.

not a few of the most vocal racists are otherwise devout churchmen and churchwomen. Not all of these invoke the Bible (quoted out of context) to justify their racial prejudices and practices, but all show a certain religious fanaticism in upholding their racist position. This is baffling, to say the least.

It seems to me quite clear that the Church should neither condemn nor condone these people without first examining what needs they are trying to satisfy in their racism. To put it candidly,* the crux of the problem lies in the fact that modern man is lost in a new, uncharted world with an ever changing, increasingly open society, in which mobility of population, both vertical and horizontal, is the normal state of affairs. Moreover, man's value in this world is increasingly measured by his productivity based on technical skill, not by his racial, or even family, background. Former landmarks and boundaries, so to speak, are missing, and many people confront this new world with the same dread with which primitive man confronted the jungle. These people are then driven to seek some readily identifiable group in which to find people of their kind with whom they can enter into a congenial and, more or less, intimate relationship without effort on either side. Racial groups—especially in the situation where one is pitted against another—seem to offer the identification and protection these people want. The rapidly emerging world society overwhelms them, and they are unable to accept it as the habitat of their souls. Accordingly, they try to create for themselves a world much smaller, cozier, and more easily manageable.

This analysis forces us to re-examine the meaning of the human group in terms of human personality and freedom. This is not a new problem. Nicholas Berdyaev devoted much

* I have dealt with this problem at length in my *Race Relations and Christian Mission* (New York: Friendship Press, 1964).

of his life to grappling with it, and before him Soren Kierke-
gaard assayed it. Many years of personal involvement in the
problems of racial and ethnic relations, however, have led me
to a fresh appreciation of the significance of small groups
with which an individual identifies in terms of the assertion
of his identity as a person and his acceptance by others. Here
it is easy to see how a group, racial or otherwise, may contain
in it a seed of demonic potential. In the kind of world in
which modern man lives, it is extremely easy to absolutize
any of the more readily identifiable groups. When absolutized, such a group imprisons the individual in it, keeps him
walled in, separates him from the outer world, makes him less
a person, and ultimately smothers him to death. Far too many
people are in this predicament, hastening to finish their course
toward an unwept death as nothing else than "whitemen"!
They have saved their skin only to lose their soul.

In the light of this phenomenon, widely and intensely
experienced by modern man, the traditional doctrine of the
Church needs to be re-examined. What does it mean, em-
pirically, to say that one believes in and belongs to the one,
holy, catholic, and apostolic Church—the community of the
saints—in a world-wide, open, dynamic, and secular society,
growing both ethno-racially and religio-culturally more and
more pluralistic? How should the Church express itself struc-
turally in such a society? How can it be the Church, the
Body of the world-redeeming Christ, if it is just another in-
group (which at present it often is) for an insignificant minority group, however interracial its membership is? Theologically, besides the doctrine of the universal brotherhood of
all mankind under the fatherhood of one God and the doctrine of the inalienable value, dignity, and sanctity of every
individual person, the Church needs a doctrine of human
groups in the formulation of which the insights of the modern
social sciences are taken seriously.

Toward a New Theology of Mission and Ministry

The five issues raised and briefly discussed in the preceding pages point to the fact that the Church stands in a totally different kind of relationship to the world than it has ever had before, except during the Apostolic and immediately post-Apostolic period. The Church now is, as it then was, a "colony of heaven" (Phil. 3:19, Moffatt). That is, the Church exists in the world, for it has been sent into the world by Christ, even as Christ himself was sent into the world by God (Jn. 17:18, 20:21). This is what Hendrick Kraemer has been saying in recent years in his well-known statement "The Church is Mission."

We pointed out early in this paper that the underlying motif of mission, whether Roman Catholic or Protestant, had been "conquest": namely, Christendom conquering heathendom, the Christian gospel conquering paganism. And that being the *motif*, the Church's ministry was something to be dispensed only to those who were "insiders" of the Church, while the mission of the Church to "outsiders" was to proclaim the gospel and gain converts.

That dichotomy of mission and ministry is not tenable today. The mission and ministry of the Church in the present world are one; because the Church, in order to be the Church *within* and *in relation to* the world, is no more and no less than the mission. The Church has been sent into the secular world to remind it that the secular is an integral part of God's creation, that Christ died for its redemption, and that it is under the reign of God himself. The ministry of the Church is to equip all the saints with the Holy Spirit so that they, as the Body of Christ, may corporately share in God's own ministry to reconcile the world unto himself. This is what "ministry of the laity" ultimately is, and it is nothing new.

The biblical concept of ministry is, as it is most clearly stated in Ephesians 4:1-16, basically *corporate*, in that the task is given to the whole Church, the people of God, the new Israel. (See also 1 Cor. 12.) Thus conceived, the mission of the Church is primarily neither to bring non-Christians into the Church as converts or proselytes, nor to christianize the social order (as the Social Gospel movement used to claim), nor yet to put the secular world under the control of the Church.

What then is the mission of the Church, and how can it be fulfilled? This is the basic and central question to which the Church today must find an answer through ecumenical conversation, on the one hand, and through direct encounter with and involvement in the secular world, on the other. No individual theologian, however competent, can fully answer the question, nor can any single Christian communion. One might go so far as to say that no classical system of theology will be of much help. What is needed today, much more than anything else, is a more dynamic, functional theology that takes every existing secular discipline seriously and, through both dialogue and collaboration, tries to help modern man to perceive what God is doing in the secular world and to discover how he is to witness to what he sees God doing in his daily life and among his neighbors.*

Such a theology will come neither out of the study of the professional theologian, nor from the lecture halls of theological schools, nor from the desks of ecclesiastical bureaucrats, nor from conferences. It will only be born out of honest and serious confrontation of theologians with Christians engaged in secular occupations. It will come not from

---

* Two significant study documents have been published by the World Council of Churches on these questions: *The Missionary Task of the Church: Theological Reflections* (Division of Studies Bulletin VII-2); and *A Theological Reflection on the Work of Evangelism* (Department on Studies in Evangelism).

theological discussions per se, but rather when both begin to think theologically on worldly matters—politics, economics, education, recreation, finance, medicine, and the rest—and begin to discover together what God is doing in one and all of these areas of human society. In this joint enterprise, theologians of professional competence are indispensable; but they need men and women from all walks of life as joint participants. Neither side is exclusively to teach the other, but both sides must listen to and learn from each other. It is of the greatest importance that the integrity of every discipline be fully respected in this process of mutual and common learning and growing together.

How can this be brought about and carried out? Enthusiasm alone will not do. What is essential, but what we do not yet have, is a common conceptual frame of reference within which specialists of the highest competence in their professional disciplines can engage in dialogue with one another. It seems to me that the Anglican tradition of incarnational and sacramental theology, not as a system of creedal tenets, but as a basic outlook on the reality of God's created world and everything therein, may make a unique contribution in terms of providing an intellectual climate and a frame of reference in which this interdisciplinary conversation may take place. Such conversations have not thus far been undertaken and tested, but it may well be the challenge which Anglican theological circles can ill afford to evade.

2

J. Lynn Leavenworth:

Do the Baptists Have Treasures?

Baptists in America have been so preoccupied guarding what they suppose is a precious church treasure, a regenerate church membership, that they have given only feeble attention to ecumenical discussions. Most church-union movements have swiftly passed them by. Sometimes they wonder if the treasure they have so zealously guarded is still there.

During the past decade, there have been such bold, almost reckless, sorties into ecumenical confrontations and actual church mergers! And this on the part of staid church bodies, supposedly too embedded in tradition to move beyond a snail's pace. It has confused the Baptists. Just as that body of Free Churchmen was getting used to the idea of acknowledging any historical antecedents to their present at all, suddenly the air is full of ecumenical and church-union talk. And on top of it all, comes the Second Vatican Council, with its call for reform and renewal and its implicit challenge to Protestantism to put its own house in order if there is to be a season of conversation.

Over the years it has been so much easier for Baptists

to suppose they were being authentic in their reliance upon
the Scriptures when they were stating their distinctive slogans
than it was to doggedly work at the hard task of articulating
the theological understanding of their existence. Thus it is
not surprising to find other church bodies relatively uninter-
ested in the repetition of "freedom of conscience," "the ministry of the laity," "the priesthood of all believers," "the
autonomy of the local church," and "the separation of Church
and state." It is discomfiting to hear pronouncements in these
very areas, in forceful manner and compelling logic, by
spokesmen of the very churches that were considered by Free
Churchmen to be disablingly encumbered by the weight of
institution, impossibly checkreined by episcopacy, and suffocated by the dusty layers of dead creed.

Surely the Church must be exploring the ways to meet
the changing world. While Baptists are trying to decide
whether or not to respond to the commission to be the
church in the world, to meet the Lord Christ there, it is confusing to see those churches once considered bound and imprisoned not only freed but eagerly running to the edges of
the parish to find footing for the creation of new structures
in the dynamic culture.

There are sole, individual Baptists standing in company
with all of the creative activities implied above. There is,
however, a stubborn reluctance on the part of the Baptists as
a denominational body to put the old faith into confessional
structures, to say nothing of seeking an articulation of the
new. They have an inherent dread of statements that may
seem to be binding on individuals or churches. Consequently,
it has proven almost impossible for Baptists to be represented
in any official manner in ecumenical discussion or church-
movement explorations. Able individuals are frustrated when
repeatedly they are forced to speak only as "individual Baptists."

It is the thesis of this paper that when Baptists do break out of their hypnotic fascination with the fruit of their sixteenth- and seventeenth-century forefathers and begin creatively to explore their so-called "distinctiveness," they are delighted to find there the bedrock of catholicity which is the same bedrock that makes any serious ecumenical conversation authentic. It will be the task of the paper to sum up some of the difficulties Baptists face as they approach ecumenical conversations, and to indicate encouraging signs of theological renewal taking place among them. In this there is some promise of a more significant role for Baptists in such ecumenical discussions.

"Peculiar" Baptist Doctrines?

Of course, Baptists have no doctrines that are peculiar to themselves. In respect to the fundamentals of the Christian faith, they stand in the mainstream of Christian tradition. A Baptist historian, Robert G. Torbet, insisted on this when he said that Baptists in the final analysis are "Protestants who hold in common with other Christians the great doctrines of the faith as set forth in historic Christianity." [1] He echoes the testimony of most students of Baptist origins and life.

That is not to say that the concerns traditionally associated with them are not useful in characterizing Baptists. On the contrary, their persistent defensiveness in regard to these concerns, centering as they do primarily in a regenerate and mission-obedient church membership, may be their identifying mark. It is not that any one of the concerns is unique to Baptists, but that together they represent key points in the struggle to maintain a responsible church body.

Maring and Hudson, in their *Baptist Manual of Polity and Practice*, speak of the confusion in identifying the characteristic marks of Baptists by saying:

A typical list of Baptist distinctives is apt to include the following points: the Scriptures, or the New Testament, as the supreme authority for faith and practice; the priesthood of believers; freedom of conscience, soul liberty, and the right of private interpretation; congregational polity; the autonomy of the local church; believer's baptism by immersion; and a regenerate church membership.[2]

Then they add, "Some of them are not so much distinctive of Baptists as they are beliefs of Protestants in general. Others are distortions of some valid Baptist emphases. A few are closely related to the true genius of Baptists." [3] This "genius" is not well defined in the *Manual*, but the authors find that believer's baptism is "significant" both from a theological and a practical point of view.[4] It is obvious that this view of baptism is not exactly unique with the denomination. Not only are there other church bodies that practice believer's baptism, but eminent theologians of traditionally pedobaptist churches, such as Emil Brunner and Karl Barth, have come to the concept as a logical conclusion of their studies of the nature of the Church.*

Even if these "distinctives" are not technically so distinctive, Baptists have frequently removed themselves from church-union discussions, or have not been invited to them in the first place, when these concerns appear threatened. Dr. Torbet affirms that Baptists in conversation with other Christian bodies will not accept concepts that imply deviations from the following Baptist positions: "(1) the recogni-

---

* An excellent summary of the gradual involvement of world-wide Baptists in the ecumenical discussions of baptism, springing up as a result of questions raised by Brunner and Barth, may be found in an article by the British Baptist, Ernest A. Payne: "Believers' Baptism in Ecumenical Discussion," *Foundations*, January, 1960, pp. 32 ff. Another summary in the same issue of *Foundations*, written by Reidar B. Bjornard, "Important Words on Baptism from Continental Protestants," illustrates this further.

tion of an establishment (i.e., a state church); (2) the subordination of ministers and churches to an episcopacy, under which ordination and church authority are vested in bishops; (3) the adopting of a creed binding upon the consciences of believers; (4) a compromise of the New Testament principle of believer's baptism." [5]

Historical Memories

Baptists, like other churchmen, carry denominational memories, predispositions, and concerns to the tables of ecumenical discussion. Frequently, for Baptists, these become entangling encumbrances, due to the paradoxes and contradictions of that history.

The Baptists have English origins in the seventeenth-century separatist tradition of the Puritan movement. There they learned an earnestness about the purity of the church congregation. There, too, they learned to make clear definitions of position in the context of the lively discussions and disputes of the time. In the process of developing a radical protection of the church as a body of faith and mission, the Baptists practiced clear articulation and definition.

If this were the whole memory, the case would be simple today. Nineteenth-century America altered the situation. Across the "frontier" territories of America during that century, Baptists multiplied and flourished at a phenomenal rate. The motivations were based on the strong passions of pietism and "missions." In the process, "experience" was substituted for rational statement as a criterion for a valid Christianity. This emphasis upon experience, coupled with individualism, prevailed until the breath of modern thought in the late nineteenth and early twentieth centuries chilled the ardor.

From the beginning Baptists had protected the "freedom of conscience" by insisting that a creedal statement was to be used only for the purpose of definition, teaching, and witness-ing; it could never be binding on fellow believers. However, during controversies in the early decades of the twentieth century, creeds were used negatively to attack the prevailing thought and practices of the denomination. Increasingly the American Baptist Convention turned to "Christian experi-ence" or the "sole authority of the Scriptures," avoiding any kind of creedal statement. Thus the early memory of the need to define the Baptist position for the purposes of self-identity and apologetics was overlaid with a disposition to re-ject all creedal statements and formulations.

There is a further difficulty in the very complexity of Baptist groups. Even though the Baptist World Alliance, organized in 1905, includes the many major bodies of Baptists in the United States and around the world, these bodies are diverse in thought and temper. The Southern Baptist Con-vention rejects all ecumenical relationships; the American Baptists have normal membership and leadership in the vari-ous councils of churches; the National Baptist Conventions are unstructured and tend to be highly emotional; the Union of Great Britain and Ireland is characterized by order and in-tellectual discipline. The Baptist World Alliance provides fel-lowship, service, and co-operation among these but "may in no way interfere with the independence of the churches or assume the administrative functions of existing organiza-tion." [6]

This is only part of the background for the confusing, self-contradictory memories Baptists bring to the discussion tables. To sum up, there is the memory of clear, disciplined statements and the memory of non-rational experience as a criterion; the memory of solidarity of viewpoint and mission, and the memory of splintering and dissension; the memory of the importance of community in Christian interpretation, and the memory of naked individualism; the memory of a shared theological heritage in the Reformed tradition, and the memory of an audacious self-confidence that Baptists above all others represent a pure New Testament church.

However, with the rising tide of denomination-wide theological studies, conferences, and publications since the middle of the twentieth century, Baptists are discovering a broad catholicity in their concept of the church as a body of believers drawn together in the bonds of Christ. A new mood of inquiry, study, and articulation is motivating Baptists to understand themselves and to participate in ecumenical discussions.

Major Issues Involving Baptists

What are the major issues for Baptists at the forefront of the ecumenical discussions? The problem of "authority" remains as unfinished business for Baptists. Of course, Baptists are true children of the Reformation in their recognition of Jesus Christ as the ultimate authority, and in the recognition of the "indubitable authority" of the Bible.[7] This in itself presents a constant problem of interpreting the Scriptures. Fortunately, the Baptists today have moved beyond the initial negative reactions to biblical criticism.* They are now grappling fundamentally with problems of hermeneutics and exegesis, taking in stride the tools of modern scholarship. There is no question that this will continue to demand the consistent efforts of the total community of Christian scholars, composed of all branches of Christianity. In this context it

* It is this author's observation that few Baptist seminaries feel any restraint in their Bible departments from entering wholeheartedly into the discussions of Bultmann, Dibelius, Cullmann, et al. However, this is not to say that Baptist pastors and laymen are completely supportive. Especially in the South there have been marked tensions between seminary faculties and boards of control over what is regarded as the excessive critical approach to the Scriptures on the part of the faculty, especially in their published work.

has been refreshing for Baptists to discover that there is a whole Bible, an Old Testament as well as a New Testament. This has corrected a tendency toward highly selective dependence upon portions of the New Testament only. Scholars approaching the Scriptures in the context of such discussions have noted that the apology for many of the Baptist "distinctives" has depended unduly on limited strands of scriptural material. This has led to painstaking examinations of the total Bible in response to the revelation of God.

Baptists and Tradition

These are serious matters. Even so, they do not represent the central problem for Baptists in regard to authority. That problem has to do with tradition. The time has come for a frank re-facing of the role of tradition in authority. Dr. Harrelson intimates this when he discusses the need for understanding the two Testaments in their interrelationships and in their combined impact "in the light of (1) careful examination of the precise meaning of the text; (2) the guidance of the Holy Spirit; (3) *the corporate witness of the church across the centuries;* and (4) our own growing experience as obedient followers of him who is both Light and Life." [8]

While this would be regarded as a feeble gesture by most major Christian bodies, it suggests a radical rethinking for Baptists. In this century particularly, there has been an automatic reflex of dismissal of "tradition" as being anti-Baptist. This has occasioned uneasiness and withdrawal from involvement with those Christian bodies who acknowledge dependence upon tradition. Baptists, through automatic dismissal of the subject, were assuming incorrectly that it was possible to develop theological concepts without the recognition of tradition.

Harrelson, in the essay cited above, brings forcibly to

the attention of Baptists the need to articulate an understanding of the interdependence of faith and reason as conditions for the very existence of the community of faith. He traces the Baptist factions that have at one time accented one or the other of these points of tension. "Until faith and reason get together with some degree of unanimity, the authority of the Scriptures will be compromised and impoverished." [9] Tracing the dependence of faith and reason in the very formation of the Scriptures themselves, in the recovering of the revelation regardless of the historical era, Harrelson proceeds to discuss the "Authority and Place of Creeds and Confessions" among Baptists. Although he considers these as "pæans of praise," "banners of the faith," and short definitions for the instruction of new members, he places the question of the role of tradition before the "Bible-loving" Baptists. In doing this, of course, he emphatically dismisses the use of any summary formulation of the historic faith to construct "instruments of coercion and proscriptions of belief."

Baptists face the fundamental problem of understanding their own Free Church tradition with its unwritten (but often rigid and doctrinaire) theology, and also of understanding their own continuity with the great affirmations imbedded in the tradition of the total Christian body from the third century to the sixteenth. It is a rare member of a Baptist congregation who has any familiarity with the Apostles' Creed, the Nicene Creed, or any other historic formulation. But it is not so rare to hear Baptists speak of the Triune God, the dual nature of Christ, the eschatological hope of the Church, in terms shaped by these historic formulations.*

---

* There are few Baptist theologians today who would trace the "tradition" of the Baptists back through the successive generations of non-conformists and heretics to the first-century separation from the "orthodox" Jewish body. An experienced Baptist speaker, however, is never surprised to find important Baptist laymen who vaguely suppose something of that sort is the truth, or that the origins lie in the ministry of John the Baptist.

Frankly facing the relationship of Scriptures and tradition as related to the authority of Jesus Christ over the community of believers is a necessity for their survival as a Christian community. It is also a preparation for ecumenical discussions. Barrenness, or complete absence, of responsible theological construction will be the result of ignoring this relationship. Baptists do have a theological outlook, whether or not it is admitted. It is not possible to turn from a serious view of history and tradition (in the interest of asserting sole dependence upon the Scriptures) without being vulnerable to influences that are strictly sociological and historical in nature. When such relativities are identified critically with the "Word of God," the spiritual life of the church becomes imprisoned, suffocated, lost. It results in the ignorant (yet sinful) rejection of God's will for his people.

Two helpful lines of development give promise in this respect. First, the necessity of understanding the Scriptures through dependence upon historical and personal perspectives provides Baptists with an opening to a dynamic understanding of tradition. Problems of canonization, historic corrections of heretical movements, and the history of hermeneutics have increasingly drawn the attention of Baptist scholars. One Ph.D. candidate has chosen patristics as his field of concentration, and is developing a thesis (a rugged one for Baptists) that one cannot properly approach the Reformation at all without a command of the patristic materials. He—somewhat tentatively—is exploring the idea that the very heart of the Baptist witness to a regenerate church membership has its formative stages in that period.

Another opening to tradition comes naturally from dependence upon the Holy Spirit for the revelation of the Word through the words of the Scriptures. Logically, the study of the Holy Spirit in relation to the interpretation of Scripture for the twentieth-century man leads to the con-

sideration of God's will seen in the direct leading of th
Spirit.

Baptists, in the Calvinist tradition, have avoided the ex
cesses of the extreme left-wing reformers who embraced a
antinominal irrationalism, in the interest of holding to the d
rect revelation and enlivening action of the Holy Spirit. I
is the claim of the modern descendants of the Anabaptis
that their forebears in Reformation times were to be distir
guished from the "spiritualists" at that very point: the Ana
baptists were "biblicists" who "remain as close as possible t
the Bible, whereas the spiritualists value the immediate illum
nation by the Holy Spirit higher than the revelation in th
Word." [10]

To repeat, the historical descendants of the Regul:
Baptists of England have always held the Holy Spirit, th
Bible, and the Lordship of Jesus Christ in an inseparabl
union as they have approached the problem of authority
However, most of the attention has been given to the Bibl
and the person of Christ. Maintaining a firm anchorage i
the historically unique revelation of Jesus Christ as reveale
through the Scriptures, the development of the doctrine c
the Holy Spirit cannot help but enlarge the Baptist view c
the revelatory role of history and tradition in understandir
the authoritative Word of God.

As this process develops, the barriers will be lowered be
tween the Free Churches and the churches in other tradition

Ecclesiology

Ecclesiology and church polity, of course, represent a
area of distinctives for Baptists. The insistence upon a reger
erate church membership, and the various means of guardir
that understanding of the nature of the Church certainly pro
vide the keys to the Baptist "treasures." As is indicate

hroughout this paper, the doctrine of the Church has been under constant study by Baptists. They have been forced into this re-examination by the thrust of the theological times. When Baptists read Emil Brunner's *Misunderstanding of the Church*,[11] or John Knox's *The Church and the Reality of Christ*[12] or the volumes stemming from the various Faith and Order discussions,[13] or any of the constant flow of volumes and articles during the past two decades on the nature of the Church, the experience comes as a triple revelation: How often one encounters emphases that Baptists supposed they alone were protecting; how poorly Baptists are prepared to speak at this high level of articulation; how badly Baptists need the stimulation of these earnest efforts to understand the nature of a responsible Church of Jesus Christ.

Most of the Baptist studies of the biblical base of the doctrine of the Church are not distinguishable as "Baptist." There may be some preference for the concept of the "people of God" rather than the "Body of Christ" in tracing the biblical materials, but this in no wise constitutes a peculiar "Baptist" stamp. Probably the major problem for Baptists comes not at the theological understanding of the Church so much as in the development of the polity of the denominational life. Although each of the concepts that can be mentioned as "Baptist distinctives" has had its direct appeal to Scriptures, it appears altogether possible that most of them are in the realm of polity and may, indeed, be forged out of the relativities of ecclesiastical adjustments and reforms.

Winthrop Hudson has termed it "Stumbling into Disorder" and states the need for reorganization rather bluntly: "Chaotic may be too strong a word to use in describing the denominational structure of the Baptists, but there are few who will deny that there is confusion and disorder. . . . Since a major obstacle to any attempt to make some sense of our denominational relationships is the rather widespread be-

lief that the present structure is in some way derived from
New Testament precepts, or at least from historic Baptist principles, it is important to point out that this is *not* true. Our
denominational structure has not been the product of biblical,
theological, or even rational considerations." [14] He goes on
to show the results of sectional and partisan pressures and the
need for money-raising efficiency. The "stumbling into disorder" occurred when, in the early part of the nineteenth
century, Baptists rejected an organization "composed of delegates from the various Associations" and chose instead to develop one "composed of individuals who contributed to its
funds. . . ." [15] Thus was formed the basis for the national
boards and agencies (Foreign Mission Society, Home Mission
Society, Publication Society, Educational Societies, etc.)
which to this day represent an impossible barrier to an or-
derly ecclesiastical structure.

Over the years improvements have been made in the
organizational relationships, bringing increased efficiency.
Thus when the American Baptist Convention was formed in
1907 (then "Northern" Baptist Convention), it was to cen-
tralize fund-raising and effect co-operative program-planning,
but it did not disturb the underlying autonomy of the local
church. Despite the present-day efforts to provide a more
logical and efficient organization along the lines recom-
mended by business management consultants, the denomination falls short of a suitable church body. Maring and Hudson write:

The reorganization plan of 1961 provided for more effective co-
operation among the various agencies of the denomination, and
the increased size of the General Council makes possible a more
representative expression of opinion with regard to its decisions
The churches which are supposed to be the real source of authority, however, lack adequate channels through which to express
their will with regard to issues and policies, and the national con-

vention in the annual session is too unwieldy to serve as a deliberative body. . . . Also it is necessary to define more specifically and delegate more formally the authority of those in executive posts, thus legitimizing for each whatever power he should rightly exercise. The only way in which these ends can be achieved is through a truly representative church polity.[16]

It may be seen from the above that the barriers to ecumenical conversations (or even church union) may not be so high as either Baptists or non-Baptists suppose. Naturally this does not mean that any conversations of a serious kind will be easy, but it could mean that at least the formal reasons for not considering such conversations may be removed. As Baptists begin to move with more self-assurance and preparation into faith-and-order discussions, there is no question that a true community of research and study across confessional lines can be quickly realized.

Adult Baptism

But what about baptism? Not only has the practice of the baptism of believers given the denomination its name, but probably most people would consider the rite, and perhaps the mode of immersion, as being the chief identifying mark of the group. While Baptists normally would derive their concept of baptism from their doctrine of regenerate church membership, baptism does play an extremely important part in the life of the congregation. But here, and in the case of the Lord's Supper, there is considerable confusion.

For the most part, studies show that there has been little theological study of either of the sacraments among Baptists. The major Baptist groups divide in their approach to the rites. The practice of "alien Baptism" (that is, the refusal to recognize the validity of baptisms, even by immersion, when conducted by other than "true" church) is widespread among the Southern Baptists, but rare among the American Baptists. The same may be said for "closed communion" (the practice of admitting only truly baptized members of the particular church to the Lord's Table). Such practices have erected impossible barriers to all ecumenical discussions and fellowship. Often they are applied even to members of other Baptist bodies. That these are extreme emphases, and an embarrassment to most theological leaders in the South, is obvious as one talks with such individuals in theological conferences.

Nonetheless, both American and Southern Baptists share the need for a thorough re-examination of both sacraments. T. C. Smith, writing then as a Southern Baptist, in his essay on the "Doctrine of Baptism in the New Testament" judged that the Baptists were true to the New Testament in their practice of baptism but that "very little emphasis has been placed . . . on the meaning of baptism for those who submit to it. There is great need for a more thorough study of the biblical evidence which must form the foundation for a more adequate theology of this Christian rite." [17]

As he himself attempts this New Testament study, he quickly passes beyond the normal Baptist assertion of baptism as a simple obedience to a command of Jesus to baptize. He sees the meaning as unity with Christ, and the re-enactment of what happened to Christ. While for him baptism never becomes an instrument of salvation, he does see that in the rite the believer participates in the work of Christ and receives the benefit of the victory.

Norman Maring, in reviewing the significant book by Markus Barth, *Die Taufe—Ein Sakrament?* (*Baptism—a Sacrament?*—Evangelischer Verlag, 1951), states that "If this book had been written by a Baptist, its conclusion would occasion no surprise. Indeed, it supplies the solid biblical and theological foundations for the doctrine of believers' baptism which Baptist scholars have neglected to provide." [18] It is reported that in that book Barth finds that "both implicitly and explicitly he asserts that baptism is not to be regarded as a 'means of grace.' The only thing which can legitimately be considered as a means of grace . . . is the work which has been wrought in the death and resurrection of Jesus Christ." [19]

Just such a book by Baptists as Maring called for was produced by a group of British Baptists in 1959, *Christian Baptism*.[20] This book focuses attention upon the central issue of whether baptism is to be understood as man's response to the mercies of God, in which the baptized dramatically conveys his repentance, humility, obedience, and faith, or whether it is an even deeper drama in which both God and man act. Does the baptized receive in baptism the gift of the Holy Spirit, is he united to Jesus Christ, and is he received into the Body of Christ, the Church?

One of the writers, Neville Clark, states that "Baptism . . . implies, embodies, and effects forgiveness of sin, initiation into the church, and the gift of the Holy Spirit." [21] This incorporation into the community of the risen Lord, the true Israel, remains in eschatological tension, because the Christ who has come remains the Christ who will come. Baptism is Christological; it is baptism into Christ, "into the crucified, risen, and ascended Lord, into the whole drama of his redemption achievement." [22] He emphasizes that the term "into Christ" is an incorporation into the whole Christ, "*Totus Christus*," into the whole head and members.

As to who the "rightful recipients of baptism" may be, Dr. Clark reviews the scriptural base dispassionately and concludes that the accent on adult baptism may have been the logical outcome of the first generation of Christians, being in a new missionary situation. It is interesting to note that he concludes that "the way ahead lies in the recognition that the overriding appeal must always be to New Testament theology rather than to New Testament practice." [23] As he seeks this

theological ground, he looks to the baptism in Jordan with
its fulfillment in the cross, resurrection, and ascension rather
than looking to the incarnation for his clue. And yet baptism
is not to be effected "over the head of man." There is a con-
junction of divine action and human response which can
never be denied. The rite of baptism can never be understood
as associated with "racial succession," but remains always as
Heilsgeschichte ("the history of salvation"), the gradual
formation and development of God's chosen people in history.

Dr. Clark places his finger on another sensitive spot for
Baptists when he challenges the idea of the necessity of faith
inasmuch as baptism in the New Testament remains "a sacrament of the Gospel, not of our experience of it; of God's
faithfulness, not of our faithful response to him. . . ." [24] To
insist upon prior individual acts of faith is to disregard the
continuity of sacred history, and it tends to overstate the
"rich flowering of the recognition of individual personality"
from the primitive ideas of collectivism.[25] Baptism always
points beyond itself for movement, because it is a sign of both
fulfillment and unfulfillment. "Our redemption was accomplished at the cross and resurrection; it is accomplished at
baptism; it will be accomplished at the *parousia*."

Persistently the author probes areas of weakness. For example, he comments on the practice of "blessing of infants" in
recent years among Baptists. He relates this to the practice
of infant baptism which, he says, historically has been in
search of a theology to support the practice. For him such a
search must lead to a balancing of the objective and subjective elements in redemption—the Word that calls to Spirit
and the Spirit that responds to Word. In that divine dialogue,
room will be provided "for man to find his freedom in a surrender which is truly his own." [26]

As to the mode of baptism, he is certain that when immersion as a mode is made obligatory, it is without warrant.

But he insists that the constant practice of affusion must be questioned.

This kind of inquiry into baptism is far beyond the preparation of most Baptists in the United States, but it is an effort of the British Baptists to open windows toward the current theological discussions of the sacraments among all Christian bodies. In the process it reveals the barrenness of the practice of the rite by those who pay so little attention to the meanings. As George Younger commented in his editorial introductions to the January, 1960, issue of *Foundations* (which was devoted to the subject of baptism), Baptists have done little more than stick a hesitant toe into the ecumenical conversations. "If, when meeting among themselves in the Baptist World Alliance, they have produced little solid agreement, it is not surprising that their informal and partial participation in faith-and-order discussions has had so little effect." [27] He points out that when the churches have such varying understanding of what they are doing when they are baptizing, even according to believers' baptism by immersion, it is folly to insist that God's grace is truly operative wherever these "proper" conditions are met, or that God's grace is not operative when other conditions are practiced.

A "Problem" with the Lord's Supper

It was extremely interesting to note the problem faced by the Jesuit scholar Michael J. Taylor when he wrote his book *The Protestant Liturgical Renewal*.[28] The book grew out of an extensive survey study of various representative Protestant bodies, including the Baptists. As he examined the returned questionnaires and reviewed the mass of interview notes, he found it impossible to discuss the Baptists in a manner parallel to the other major denominations. Liturgy for him meant the form and content of external worship. He focused sharply on the development of Protestant thought concerning the Eucharist. Among the Baptists, he chose to approach only pastors of the American Baptist Convention. From the very first returns he saw that no follow-up of the Baptists would be needed, because "it was apparent from the first response that the subject of our study was not of immediate and practical concern to pastors in this church." [29] In the nine chapters of the book, he discusses his findings among the Protestant churches. He concludes:

Despite the general unwillingness to associate in any real sense the unique sacrifice of Christ with the Lord's Supper, a growing number of Protestants speak of the Eucharistic rite as an *anamnesis* of Christ's original Sacrifice, namely, a sacramental *summoning present* of the unique sacrifice of Christ, at least in the sense that its fruits are made real and present to us in the Sacrament. [30]

But where then are the Baptists? Dr. Taylor found it necessary to relate his findings about them in an "Appendix on the Baptists." There he demonstrates a remarkably fair objectivity in stating what he found, and what he had read in a very adequate bibliography. [31] His summary description of Baptists is interesting:

The Baptist is a Christian not because he is a member of a Christian Church but because he has accepted the absolute lordship of Jesus Christ, whose life and redeeming message are unfolded for him in the Bible. If he has a norm for religious action, an authority to govern him, a creed to teach him, it is the Bible, illumined by the light of the Spirit. The Baptist, armed with the Bible and guided by the Spirit, exercises supreme responsibility over his own soul before God and believes that no state, or religion, or group of ecclesiastics should dictate to him the religious principles that are to govern his life. He is a free soul under God and balks at anything or anyone that might compromise that freedom. Among Christians he stands out as the 'rugged individualist,' the 'priest unto himself,' the 'spiritual nonconformist.' [32]

This apt description may generate honest pride in many Baptists, who do not distinguish between a general historical summary of a "Baptist figure" and the actual situation of Baptist men and women today who carry the banners but may have forgotten the significations and may be blind and deaf to the rapidly changing conditions of life around them.

After noting that Baptists as a church-minded people are fervent and regular in the practice of both baptism and the Lord's Supper, Dr. Taylor examines their attitude toward the two sacraments. He fastens upon the commemorative function of the ordinance of the Eucharist, following the lead of individuals (identified in the footnotes) who do not necessarily stand in the line of reinterpretation of the sacraments. He concludes that, "apart from obedience, fellowship, and commemoration, the rite has no objective purpose." However, he found that more than half of the Baptists expressed a personal interest in the liturgical revival, and a third of the total number agreed that the Word should have as its normal complement the celebration of the Lord's Supper.[33]

There is no shadow of a doubt in this writer's mind that what Dr. Taylor found in regard to Baptist understandings and practice of the sacraments may also be found in regard to the ministry, the question of freedom of conscience, and even the question of the relationship of Church and state. Baptists simply have too long assumed that they had an important, different, authentic word to say to all Christian bodies. In reality they have neglected their studies. They come tongue-tied to the seminar room. There they are either characterized, somewhat generously, as eccentric individualists, or they are by-passed as hopelessly irrelevant to the ecumenical conversations.

Yet there remains a pulsing catholicity about the Baptist witness that needs to be articulated. The insistence upon the ministry of the people of God, obedient to the mission of Christ, having a visible, historical being in this world, may well be fundamental to the nature of the Christian Church. The ease with which Baptists can move from the ecclesiastical encumbrances to a direct probing of the theological understanding of the human community and the Body of Christ can well be the envy of many churches.

And yet it depends upon the Baptists themselves. As they patiently build and rebuild the theological foundations of their Christian existence as a church body, and as they shatter the illusion that their polity and belief are identical with New Testament prototype, they can be on the way to creative articulation and ecumenical exchange. This would appear an inescapable commitment for a people holding, as the Baptists do, to the principle of the church as God's gathered people, a regenerate membership responsive to the will of God in Jesus Christ. Coupling this with the fundamental concept that there is but one Church and one people whom God has called into being, the logic leading to informed involvement is plain. Probably that involvement, based on the principles understood by the Baptists, would lead to involvement, in manners yet to be explored, with the greater community of humanity whether or not it is related to the traditional church structures.

In any ensuing conversations between Baptists and other Christian bodies, benefits mutually advantageous to all can be expected. Perhaps, after all, in such ecumenical discussions American Baptists may grow more confident that they indeed have treasures to share, that they have not been guarding mere banners of the past. As discipline is gained for the involvements with other Christian bodies and with the secular world, the treasures may consist of a series of Christian insights and commitments:

1. Upholding the faithfulness of Jesus Christ as revealed in the Scriptures.

2. The unity of the divine initiative and the human re-sponse under the conditions of freedom of conscience (soul liberty) as a true threshold to the community of faith, the regenerate church membership.

3. The normative solidarity of the entire Christian body in Jesus Christ as the reality to which all confessional and creedal formulations point, and by which they must be judged.

4. The enriching variations of worship and liturgical ex-pressions of the praise and service of God.

5. The status of the ordained ministry derived from the total ministering body of the community of faith.

It is not, of course, a matter of "sharing" treasures in the sense of passing them out. These treasures were never a private possession in the first place. The hope of earnest Baptists, as they seek the meanings of their own existence, is one of discovery: the discovery of the verities of the Chris-tian faith, and of that fundamental union in Jesus Christ, the bedrock of the universal Church. In that hope there is risk, even a willingness to gain or to lose self-identity, to the honor and glory of God in Christ.

3

Lawrence L. Durgin:

Christ Has Set Us Free

The present ecumenical climate is the product of a century of effort. The Christian Associations (Young Men's and Young Women's) and the World Student Christian Federation are the pioneers. Much later the Protestant and Eastern Orthodox communions came together in the World Council of Churches. Now with the impact of Vatican Council II, and especially the gracious prodding of Professor Hans Küng, the situation requires a new candor between Roman and non-Roman brethren. Anything less would be a rebuff to the invitation of contemporary Catholicism and a violation of the Ecumenical Movement, which is no longer in its infancy.

We can be grateful that the call to continuing reformation pushes us back to some theological essentials which have been somewhat obscured by the sociological preoccupation of recent years, a preoccupation symptomatic of a general unease in Protestantism. We are, to be sure, suffering a sociological malaise. We are organized denominationally and, in America at any rate, interdenominationally to the point of multiple taxation of resources—of personnel, finance, and patience. We have contributed to the founding of churches and the erection of buildings in the heart of ghettos—in the slum and its twin, the suburb—instead of insisting on more creative borderland locations. We have multiplied staff and exalted the specialist's role to the point where one outstanding Protestant warns against becoming clergy-ridden. But theological insistence may yet save us where sociological analysis cannot or will not.

Candor imposes two obligations—the obligation to deal with the embarrassing topics in the first place, and then of course to deal with those topics as forthrightly as possible.

The United Church of Christ, for which in this instance I am an undesignated spokesman, is a union of the Evangelical and Reformed Church together with the Congregational-Christian Churches. Each denomination, as the names imply, is the result of a previous merger. This new communion is in its infancy, having been founded in 1959. It is too early to tell whether the child is to reflect the best of each heritage or the worst. At the moment the temptation to the latter seems to equal in force the aspiration to the former. Details of this struggle are not of general interest, but the warning is pertinent. A good issue is not to be taken for granted. Consummation of a merger is not the occasion for a vacation, not because either counterpart is untrustworthy, but for the reason that human nature is pervasive and is at least half and half: half hopeful and aspiring, half despairing and cynical.

This new communion has assets. Consider the theological streams represented: Luther, Zwingli, Calvin, and Wesley, as well as the strains of the Separatist, Anabaptist, and Puritan. There is a sense in which it is true to say that the principal strands of the Reformation from both sides of the English Channel are now at long last gathered up in reunion. The United Church of Christ is not being presumptuous in claiming to have laid the theological foundation for intra-

Protestant reunion if it succeeds in developing a viable and faithful theology. This union, further, represents two of the three polities: the presbyterial and the congregational.

Finally, spokesmen for this communion are fond of saying that we are a *uniting* church as well as a *united* church. That is to say, there is an explicit willingness to engage in the losing of denominational identity in any ecumenical culmination which is true to faith and culture. United Church leaders have been the first to urge an immediate consolidation of missionary function and activity on the part of the six denominations presently discussing the Blake-Pike proposals.

These, then, are the potential assets. We represent the heterogeneity of Reformation theology, and two-thirds of Christendom's polities; and we are publicly committed to denominational liquidation as long as it is responsible. It is, however, much too early to offer a critical evaluation of these assets. So I have chosen others for the purposes of this paper.

The United Church of Christ includes the heritage of the Free Church. Some of the Free Church tenets, such as the guarantee of certain powers to the local congregation to perpetuate the principle of autonomy, are written into the new constitution. The Free Church movement is well known for this and certain other principles which seem to many to be quite untenable. These are among the embarrassing topics candor requires us to consider: (1) the freedom to believe and to doubt; (2) the autonomy of the local congregation; and (3) "the priesthood of all believers."

To put it bluntly, these principles must be demonstrated as viable, and therefore assets to the growing dialogue, or else they must be discarded as the empty slogans of a bygone era and no longer relevant to the new climate of hope and exciting possibility.

The Freedom to Believe and to Doubt

There is a statue on top of the Capitol Building in Providence, Rhode Island, representing "the independent man." He stands, as it were, through good weather and bad as a reminder of one culture's idea of the epitome of freedom. Yet, with the feet locked in cement, the statue unwittingly represents the paradox of freedom. One wag, commenting on the state's political difficulties in dealing with pigeons and starlings, commented wryly that since the symbol of freedom was locked in cement, freedom itself was at the mercy of the birds.

Anyone who has lived in and with the Free Church tradition has lived with its liabilities. The freedom to believe and to doubt has been misconstrued to include an invitation to remain indifferent and an encouragement to disbelieve. It has been taken as a license to innovate without regard for either the gospel record or the developing tradition. At times the adaptation to contemporary culture has resulted in their distortion beyond recognition. It has been known to be a sloganeering camouflage for an outright irresponsibility in relation to the rest of the Christian community. On occasion it has meant freedom for the clergy alone. The layman may or may not receive from the clergyman the same freedom he is forced to grant. Two Congregational churches about a mile apart in one city a decade ago could reflect the extremes of Christendom, one almost unitarian and the other approximating evangelical catholicism and neither experiencing great anguish. When freedom becomes institutionalized, there is danger of its becoming meaningless at best and at worst its own opposite number, its own innate contradiction. The possibility of chaos and anarchy is ever with those who lay claim to freedom as a principle.

These liabilities must be confessed at the outset, else we

shall not understand the risk of the freedom involved nor the determination with which we must "stand fast" if we are to lay hold on the "freedom for which Christ has set us free" (Gal. 5:1). Nevertheless, we witness to a Gospel insistence here. If we could live with its peculiar disciplines, and within them, we could have an appropriate and viable contribution for the Church ecumenical and for the culture which is disposed to give up freedom's quest but cannot afford to.

Unless the layman is to be a pale and inferior carbon copy of the clergy, he must remain free to be a layman. He must be freed to take unto himself the sometimes crushing blows of his daily existence in wonder and in awe. and to reflect what he feels with a vulgar honesty. He must be freed to wrestle creatively with the tenets of the faith without being hampered by a terminology which seems dated to him. He must be freed for the contemporary application of the Gospel: to come to understand that adultery is flirting with his hostess behind the kitchen door; that stealing is cheating on the expense account; and that murder is participating, even though it be through acquiescence, in a political and economic order which allows rats to bite children and forces citizens into the dangerous streets to get a hearing for their grievances.

He must be freed to identify the "principalities and powers" of Scripture with the power structures, anonymous and otherwise, with which he wrestles and by which he is hounded daily. At present the average man has no alternative but to capitulate to these structures—the structures of corporate rapacity which are participated in enthusiastically by those who would not think of exhibiting any private greed— and to the practices of buck-passing, inefficiency, and duplicity.

In this struggle the layman may have to find his own way. Clergy, for the most part, live in sheltered compound even today. To be sure, they are surrounded by symptoms

f the same principalities; but because of vested interest, they
nd to diagnose those symptoms as evidence of the human
ither than of the demonic. It is difficult for clergy to iden-
fy their systems as being anything more than frustrating.
Villiam Stringfellow's report of his meeting with students
om the Business School and the Divinity School of Harvard
Iniversity on the same day illustrates both the layman's
ituteness and his need to be freed from an insulated clergy.
Ie spoke to each group about the meaning of the "principali-
es and powers." He writes: "Though the Business School
udents were not especially theologically sophisticated, and
ertainly none had been theologically trained, they displayed
1 awareness, intelligence, and insight with respect to what
rincipalities are and what are the issues between principali-
es and human beings. Yet, when the same matters had been
iscussed earlier with the divinity students, I found that most
f them felt that such terms as 'principalities and powers,'
uling authorities,' 'demons,' 'world rulers of the present
arkness,' 'angelic powers,' and the like—terms so frequently
sed in the Bible—were archaic imagery having no reference
） contemporary realities." [1]

This is not to claim that the layman left on his own is
etter off without benefit of clergy. But there is the strong
iggestion that after the layman has been informed by the
ospel, indeed while he is in the process of being informed, he
iould be freed to struggle through to the application of it on
is own, at least in part. Ministers and seminarians in their
etachment from the world *as it is* are unaware that the world
oes not have to be as it is and that in being so it has scored a
ictory against the thinking of the Church itself. The layman,
eed by the gospel from the inevitability of an ultimate vic-
ory on the part of "principalities and powers," could con-
eivably join the issue with the world *as it is* for a victory
ver the world as it *does not have to be*.

If the layman is to achieve the kind of mature courage

required, he must be permitted the freedom for a curricular doubt. Extracurricular doubt is, of course, of no value. Like extracurricular faith, it is no more than a conversation piece for the cocktail hour. Curricular doubt is another matter. From Thomas and Paul down through Augustine, gathering up learned and articulate Christians from every century through the ages, there have been countless men and women for whom curricular doubt has proved to be the proper climate ultimately for a curricular faith. The freedom to doubt may be the climate for the ringing affirmation of a mind which knows and has been tempted by the dismal alternatives and, having put them aside, is prepared to stand firm. The freedom to be selfish has given rise to the stewardship of a cheerful and decisive giver, who experiences a measure of the pain of true sacrifice. The freedom to sin can lead to the fruits of the righteousness which is of God alone, encouraging a genuine confession and sparing the sinner the hypocrisy of pretending that he does not sin.

The layman is not easily discouraged by dilemma, nor is he frustrated by paradox. On the contrary, he is discouraged by the tendency to oversimplify and the practice of solving all paradoxes by homiletic dexterity. Unless he is freed to express this discouragement and dissatisfaction, the Church will never know that it is encouraged to be, not less profound, but more, and the layman will have no idea that the gospel is indeed a saving word.

It is Paul Tillich who makes the awkward groping here truly articulate and faithful. He points to the God whose property is ultimately elusive, who defies all the neat and logical categories of man, who is very apt at any time to explode all precious notions about him. He points to the "God who appears when God has disappeared in the anxiety of doubt." [2] He has proclaimed the eternal God who upsets our too easy affirmations, bringing us rather to that brink of despair where we must have total reliance on a non-visible means of support or perish in the rubble of the dismantled constructs of a human imagination.

The constructs of our faith, though biblically inspired and traditionally tested, are finally nevertheless the product of human imagining. There must be an openness to the mysteries to which the human definitions are attempting to point. For instance, while fully agreed that the theological basis of the Church can be no less than trinitarian, we must be mindful that this concept involves a profound mystery. Man can learn this mystery by rote, and of course he should. But he cannot live by this mystery, or live in this mystery, until he has shared personally in the death and resurrection of his Lord, until he considers himself "dead to sin and alive to God in Christ Jesus" (Rom. 6:11). The layman about to become engaged in this process needs more help than can be provided by a simple didacticism. He has to be shepherded through the experience. If he is forced into believing something he does not know for himself, he may well become discouraged from trying to live with the mystery he cannot possibly know but without which he cannot possibly live as a "new creature."

Man learns by asking questions, and when the mystery is the greatest, the questions are more in number, not less. These questions should be, and must be, raised within the Church for the sake of the layman who needs exposure to the gospel and for the sake of the Church whose answers are waiting for real questions. The immense popularity of Bishop John A. T. Robinson's *Honest to God* is in part a testimony to the layman's pent-up desire to wrestle with his honest doubts within the community of faith and not outside it. I suspect that young people are not going to bring the real questions about the "new morality" and the questions raised by the "new morality" to the Church unless and until the Church exhibits an attitude hospitable to any and every question about sex, together with a guarantee of an honest answer as well as a sympathetic ear.

Just to have urged this extension of freedom to include the layman, catechumen and confirmand as well as confirmed, is to underline frequent abuse of the principle. We should be prodded by those outside into either the practice or the disavowal of this principle we have claimed historically. We must accept the challenge to work in this freedom constructively, without compromising the historic faith. It must be the "freedom for which Christ has set us free" (Gal. 5:1), else it is worthless to us and of no value to the ecumenical discussion.

P. T. Forsyth recognized the frailty of this freedom long ago and gave solemn warning:

If our first joy is to break from that corporate tradition, and start to make everything over again from the beginning, then freedom becomes a prickly, boyish, freakish, and powerless thing, weak in itself and as weakening as every irritant is. The truth that is to rule and bind the race is not to be come at by the tour de force of an individual intelligence which strains at every leash. It is but in the school of a great and old authority that we lose our egoism and find our soul and our brethren.[3]

Our freedom must usher men into the complete authority of God, or it will be the trap door to the worst possible slavery.

In the light of such great risks, it may well be asked why we continue to use the term and to insist on the practice. I have already suggested that man grows by the experience of honest doubt, and the Church can profit from knowing at first hand what the doubts are. There is one more dimension which can be mentioned. Eric Hoffer, author of *The True Believer*, is an example of self-taught brilliance. Schooled exclusively on the farm, in the mine, as a longshoreman, and in the public library, he is by his own insistence simply one of masses of people who, as he puts it, are "lumpy with talent." We must grant a hearing to these people. No man will speak unless he is encouraged by an interested silence, a manifested desire to know on the part of the listener. There are, of course, many ways to reduce a man to silence. He can be intimidated simply by the show of authority. Institutions are intimidating to many people. The establishment by some churches of coffee houses is an acknowledgment of this. On those occasions, however, when the barriers are lowered, those who have had the patience to experience a real listening to those who are culturally deprived, racially abused, and economically exploited will testify to a certain brilliance and freshness of insight not otherwise available to the culture. When this insight is refreshed and infused by the light of the gospel, the Faith is truly the victor.

Obviously, simply to enumerate the definitions of this freedom is to confess sadly the judgment implicit, from without and from within, on those of us who plead for it. In Protestantism we must either take this freedom with utmost seriousness or discard it as being a climate too vigorous for mortal man. Either the risk and the discipline of freedom must be accepted in full, or freedom has no meaning and should no longer be claimed as a viable characteristic. The risk-questions must be given complete hospitality in the Church, or the Church must cease to claim the courage to risk. I close with the challenge presented by Paul Tillich in his eagerly awaited third volume of *Systematic Theology*:

the problem is not that of doubt as a consequence of sin; the problem is that of doubt as an element of faith. And just this must be asserted from the point of view of the Protestant principle. The infinite distance between God and man is never bridged; it is identical with man's finitude. Therefore creative courage is an element of faith even in the state of perfection, and where there is courage, there is risk and the doubt implied in risk. Faith would not be faith but mystical union were it deprived of the element of doubt within it.[4]

Autonomy

It is again P. T. Forsyth who suggests that what was founded was not a group of churches, but a Church in several locations. He writes,

What the Apostles planted was not churches but stations of the Church. What the Gospel created was not a crowd of churches but the one Church in various places. What we have everywhere is the one Church of Christ put down here and there, looking out in Corinth, Ephesus, or Thessalonica. People did not go to a meeting which was on its way to become a church; they went to the Church at a certain place of meeting.[5]

The implications of this are far-reaching, and actually they are threefold rather than singular, as is too often assumed by members of the United Church and of other denominations where the outcrop of autonomy seems to be even less well anchored in the bedrock of unity.

The commonplace implication can be dismissed in a single paragraph. It is not only unfruitful but also totally unrelated to either the Gospel or historic tradition, to say nothing of being unfeasible in a society which is otherwise increasingly interdependent. This is the implication that each church is a law unto itself, without any responsibility to or for sister churches, free to carry out its own business unilaterally, and privileged despite this to claim a corporate obedience to the lordship of Jesus Christ. This interpretation is an abuse and an abasement of the principle of autonomy, having no basis either in Scripture or in responsible church practice.

The other two implications are frequently overlooked. The first is that Christ's Body is one and that the ecumenical vocation is to realize the unity already established and not to be fractured by all the pretentious misbehavior to the conrary. If the members of Christ's Body are unruly and out of concert with each other, the Body may seem grotesque and ungainly, but it is still one Body and cannot be dismembered. Unfraternal word or competitive deed may violate the unity, but the unity cannot be destroyed. The very word "reunion" is a solemn acknowledgment of a prior and present unity.

In this context the autonomy of the local congregation requires an ungrudging respect for the several orders of the clergy and a recognition of those orders, even if there can be no reciprocity at the present time or ever. It calls for rejoicing in the other's strength, encouraging the effort and abetting the purpose of all other congregations and communions. It calls for a willingness to sublimate identity for the purpose of demonstrating the integrity of the whole. J. S. Whale has written, "The œcumenical movement will be convincing only when each separate communion is prepared to give up some cherished feature of its own architecture in the interest of a great design of architectonic unity." [6]

Other communions cannot interpret the ecumenical vocation in this way. But that inability is no excuse for those who hold to the autonomy of the local congregation. The very claim we have to being the Church catholic depends upon this understanding of respectful relationship. Otherwise we are under the judgment of Paul's question, "Is Christ divided?" (1 Cor. 1:13a). The willingness to lose identity for the sake of the total integrity is a necessity for those who extend to other congregations and communions complete and full respect. The goal for such congregations is to make a contribution which is valuable but not necessarily discernible. The autonomy of the local congregation has only a peevish significance unless the same recognition is granted to all other congregations, whatever the polity or denominational affiliation.

The third implication follows. If the Church is one in the several eras and places, so must the whole Church be present in each place. There is no excuse for an American church, even in America, or—from this point of view—for a Roman church, even in Rome. To allude to the most critical American problem, there is no excuse for a white church or for a Negro church. Congregations unable or unwilling to become integrated may logically question their status as churches. To be in Christian conversation, or even tied together in the bonds of Christian sympathy with churches in other places, does not satisfy the vocation of the Church as the whole Church in any given place. If the Church in each place is to know the dilemmas of the Church in every other place, it must be confronted by those dilemmas in its own daily work and worship. The unity of such a congregation would be strained, especially in time of war and in time of racial strife. However, if strained relations are to be offered as an excuse for avoiding the universal nature of Christianity, we must go on to raise an awkward question. Can a church that has not resolved within itself the acute tensions of our time assume the right to proclaim the gospel of redemptive reconciliation to a strife-hounded world? The world can hardly profit from the pious affirmations of a contrivedly congenial people. Nor can a congenial people afford the self righteousness which results from easy affirmations.

We can consider the relation of the Church to the United Nations as an illustration. By charter and composition that organization has to operate within the context of extreme differences. As such, it needs the counsel of those who are not only aware of these differences intellectually but have lived with them existentially. Statements from a national point of view, even when they are tempered by a Christian vocabulary and informed by Christian insight, are of little help. They only serve to confirm the fractured state of the world. To a United Nations delegate the testimony of a national church belabors obvious facts, illustrates the dimensions of human sin, and could contribute to a further general discouragement. Those who labor earnestly within the realities of international division do not require any further evidence of the fact of division.

On the other hand, if the Church could take unto itself the same pain of ideological division, the irony of economic inequity, and the stubbornness of cultural alienation, it might qualify as a welcome spokesman. Progress would be very slow. The statements on policy coming from the whole Church would be few and far between, and they would be less pointed than those which can be produced by the congenial groupings. However, real progress is slow enough now, and may continue to be until advice on the human dilemma is less gratuitous and more disciplined. The world has no reason to listen to the exhortation "to love your enemy" unless the one speaking has risked the experience of doing just that, and has suffered the humiliation of abetting enemy purposes occasionally for having taken the risk.

There is little point in a segregated church speaking to the issue of integration. A heterogeneous community cannot be expected to seek leadership from a homogeneous segment of the community. In American Protestantism we have a stubborn problem right at this point. When you combine the autonomy of the local congregation, which is quite general in practice, with the development of racial ghettos several miles thick—who can suppose that Bronxville is any less a racial ghetto than Harlem?—you have a situation where it is impossible for the whole Church, as I have defined it, to exist. Certainly the members of such parishes have very little reason to speak out on this issue and perhaps others. They may have to begin to travel many miles to identify with churches having a racial and social integrity. The only alternative is for those members to succeed in integrating the housing in their neighborhoods. The same principle obtains on the denominational level. Many of us would be happier with the Blake-Pike proposals if the denominations involved were not comprised of such terribly congenial people, people who are congenial in intellectual background, economic well-being, even ethnic and racial heritage.

These implications may seem quite idealistic and, when compared to general practice, we would have to admit that they are. The idealism is, however, the only alternative to the present anarchy, naïveté, and pretentiousness which characterize the structure, and therefore the postures and pronouncements, of most local congregations. The world of thoughtful men is fully aware of dilemma. It is probably frightened enough to heed a saving word from any authentic source. There is no reason to expect such a word from people who are insulated from the dilemmas. There might be reason to expect such a word from a people who have consciously invaded the dilemmas, armed with the gospel of Christ, and are able to present credentials testifying to their having wrestled with both the dilemmas and the gospel.

The local congregation is in the front lines of contact with the world, or could be, and of course should be. It has the eyes and ears for observing the contemporary condition, and the heart to share the circumstance of confusion and despair. It is promised the faith to risk and to stand fast, both at once. However, the local congregation cannot presume to be the Church of Christ until it accepts the vocation to be the whole Church, to have gathered up within its feeling self all the ages, all the "sorts and conditions" of men. "Reverence for the solidary race" (to borrow Forsyth's phrase) is the legitimate human basis for every church of Christ. For those who hold to the autonomy of the local congregation, it becomes the essential for each gathered community. Today's climate of reformation calls upon us to reclaim this doctrine by exercising it, lest it continue to be a prideful stumbling block. One of the most humbling facts with which we in the Free Church tradition have to contend is our intrachurch organizational chaos. Free churches in free association can be an ironic threat to legitimate autonomy. In many instances a constitutional episcopacy has proved to be a more successful guarantee for the freedom of the local congregation than the sort of superintending officer who, having no powers on paper, has no restraints on paper either.

At first glance, this discussion on the autonomy of the local congregation may seem to have little if any fruitful offering to make to the dialogue. However, since there are overtones of catholicity in this point of view, even if it has been stated necessarily in parochial terms, I should like to offer a possible connection. Father Küng suggests that improved communications, and the fact that "unity is so firmly assured in the Catholic Church today that separatism is dead," [7] open up the question of authority in an interesting way. He writes: "What a wave of constructive initiatives and fruitful developments there might be in the Church today if the episcopate and the local church (of a city, a diocese, a country, a continent) could have once again a deeper significance, a greater autonomy!" [8] Moves such as this on the part of Rome, and on the other side a recaptured emphasis on the catholic dimension of Protestant autonomy, could lead to expanding areas of dialogue, however different the ideas of autonomy may have to continue to be. This would be especially possible if the Protestant congregations would continue, in the reform, insisting on the single Church in several places and ages and the whole Church in each place—which is, it seems to me, essentially a catholic understanding of the Church. I believe the dialogue would be fruitful for the continuing reformation of the "gathered people of God" under the exclusive lordship of Christ.

I cannot end this section on the autonomy of the local congregation without conveying the enthusiasm I have gained in my experience as a parish minister. The really exciting thing about the autonomy comes clear when one sees the figure of Christ in the shape of each particular and peculiar people.

Each faithful congregation is quite different from another. Each has a character all its own, even when it shares in the ministry of the same man. Each makes its own unique contribution. The several genuine manifestations of the autonomous reflection of the spirit of Christ are perfectly fascinating. When a people faithfully takes unto itself in its culture the witness of the gospel, responding to that wisdom in faith and with courage, learning to witness for it through imagination, and developing a distinctive shape in showing forth Christ's love, I see a valid definition of the Church protestant together with the Church catholic. It is only for this goal that we dare to risk the autonomy of the local congregation. For the prize of this goal the risk is, I believe, warranted.

The Priesthood of All Believers

Given the kind of freedom in which a man's mind is to be allowed to take its own time to come to serious terms with the gospel of Jesus Christ in the context of his daily work, given the autonomy of the local congregation in which the layman has to assume responsibility for decisions and intercessory relationships otherwise reserved for the hierarchy, we could reach a new understanding of "the priesthood of all believers." If we cannot arrive at a new understanding, we may as well discard the principle as a worthless, anti-Roman battle cry.

Given this kind of intellectual and institutional climate, I have known laymen to come alive in Christ. I have seen them able to transfer the competence they have already developed in their own fields to the fields of theology and liturgics in a surprisingly short time, albeit with great effort. Often they translate what they read in books into their own idiom, and the truth does not suffer from translation. Quite the opposite. The fresh language is jarring to the indifferent, and disturbing to the complacent. I have seen a group of lay-

1en in the course of eighteen months become familiar with
1e liturgical literature, then with understandable conviction
1d great courage enact the reforms indicated by the study.
have witnessed an initial skepticism transformed into a great
elieving. This sort of believing is the child of the freedom
ɔ doubt and of the responsibility which must be shouldered
1 the autonomous local congregation.

If we take seriously the priesthood of all believers, there
an be a flowering of vitality and insight comparable to the
reat theological periods of the past. Such a theology, in-
ormed by gospel and tradition and having been fashioned
rimarily by laymen, will speak cogently to the contemporary
uman condition. It is not an accident that most of the great
heologians in history have been working members of local
ongregations, and that many of them have been laymen. It
eally is an open question whether it is easier and quicker
ɔ teach theology to an intelligent worldling or to get a semi-
arian acquainted with the world. The world in all its detail
; so complex, and faith is so deceptively simple when viewed
part from the world for which it is designed. The biblical
liom is the world's idiom and is bound therefore to suffer
istortion when interpreted by men who have, in one way or
nother, resigned from the world or who have, for one reason
r another, become detached from reality. It has to be as-
umed, of course, that the layman who wants to qualify for
his new discipline will accept the theological vocation as sub-
cantially more than an intellectual exercise.

I have seen a group of laymen accept an assignment for
study of creeds, affirmations, and covenants with deliberate
eriousness, their reading of the classic literature set in exciting
ounterpoint to the idiom of contemporary life. In reacting
ɔ the simplicity inherent in the New Testament affirmation
Jesus Christ is Lord," one member of the group, fearful that
Lord" was a little archaic, wondered out loud if the best
quivalent for today might not be the still more simple "Jesus

Christ is," thus providing us with a shocking challenge to the Humanist claim. Perhaps most significant of all has been the unhurried pace of both the individual and the corporate work, the patience being evidence of respect for the disci plines of scholarship and creativity. I have reason to trust theologically the ultimate work of this group, because I re spect the process, and I know they will disqualify themselves before they will perpetrate on the congregation anything of dubious quality.

On the national level I have witnessed the excitement and the competence of laymen when, at the General Council meeting of the former Congregational-Christian Churches, the two-hour heart of the morning usually reserved for pro motion and housekeeping business was turned over to lectures by Professors Robert Calhoun, Nels Ferré, and James Gustaf son, followed by lengthy and thoughtful discussion. Com ments by correspondents for months afterwards made it quite clear that the laymen especially felt that in their listening and speaking—for many of them spoke well—they were tending to the really serious business of the church.

There is, of course, a good deal to the priesthood beyond the privilege to question, to study, and to arrive at the historic convictions, restated or not, for oneself and together with others for the congregation. There is the matter of pastoral concern and the establishment of an intercessory relationship to fellow members, to sister churches, and to the world. There is the discipline of recognizing the sacred within the profane and the profane within the sacred; of affirming with courage the sacred against the profane; then, back in the church, of defending the profane against all sacred pretensions. There is the matter of witness in the working place, the vocation of challenging the "principalities and powers," often at personal sacrifice. Greedy political and economic structures are not easily resisted. The clichés of a materialistic art and culture are often entrenched. Cultural lag as a phenomenon is not limited to the culturally deprived. There is the matter of contemplation and prayer, so very necessary to secure the lay priest in the climate for his vocation, protecting him from the subtle as well as the brutal onslaughts through bribe and threat of a society which does become demonic when effectually challenged. There is the discipline of frugality, perhaps even a twentieth-century equivalent of poverty. The lay priest must conserve if he is going to append, and with his new imagination there are bound to be strains on the private budget until stewardship takes the place of ownership.

The priesthood described in this way points to renewal for the Church, and may also offer a clue to a way to resolve the very difficult ecumenical problem in regard to ordination. In the past Free Churchmen have said, with more cleverness than wisdom, that they would be happy to submit to re-ordination in an apostolic succession as soon as it was deemed no longer a theological essential. In other words, a practical episcopacy might be tolerable if the doctrinal insistence could be compromised. I am bound to speculate on how much pride is reflected in this attitude and whether it might not be more fruitful to explore the possibility for Free Church ministers to become qualified for one of the lay orders. The vocation as a Christian does, after all, antedate the vocation in the ministry. Is there a chance that for the Free Churchman both vocations could be fulfilled in the lay brotherhood? Could not such lay brothers continue to baptize, preach, teach, march on picket lines, go to jail? In short, could they not function pretty much as they are now, and possibly even more effectively because of the greater identification? Might they not be more effective in challenging the power structures because of their engagement in them?

A grass-roots movement in liturgical reform, a necessary activity in a communion where the local church is autonomous, has produced some surprises. It has insisted, for instance, that the reading and preaching of the Word is to be done only by those who are competent by training as well as by spirit to read and to preach. It insists that the cultural alienation from the Scriptures is so extreme that only those thoroughly acquainted with the Scriptures have any hope of reading with an understanding sufficient to induce listening, to say nothing of comprehension. There are certain functional disciplines required for "rightly handling the word of truth" (2 Tim. 2:15c). Such functional disciplines, so the reasoning goes, would be a time-consuming imposition out of all proportion on a person who is either untrained or even just out of practice. As a matter of fact, this redefinition of the role of preaching puts a strain on sermon preparation which simply did not exist when the sermon was thought to be a homily on a general truth. Such an interpretation exposes the preacher to people who have been battered by their experience during the past week in the world, battered in part because they had been encouraged the previous Sunday to charge the fortress with their aggressive defenses down. There the people are, waiting for the living and powerful Word of God, a Word with which they may face the world again and without which, if the preacher should fail on that day, going back into the world will be tantamount to suicide for the "new creature" and an open invitation for the reinstatement of the "first Adam."

Such an emphasis on the Word may seem like typical Protestantism, and to this point it is, except for the fact that what the layman thinks of as preaching has no relation to the sort of preaching which was all too prevalent prior to the impact of the Barthian protest.

What is to be said for the sacrament which, in the best years of the Church's life, has always been considered twin to the Word? The preacher who is called by the congregation to preach with such urgency week after week is keenly aware of failure and could not himself face the responsibility or the people except that he and they are bound together in the sacramental view and practice of life. The Eucharist is demanding enormous attention in this grass-roots reform. The sacrament is not to be separated from the Word, just as it cannot survive the decline inevitable without the Word. If we are to be spared the "tyranny of the pulpit," "the objective word of the sacrament" must overshadow or at least challenge "the exposition of the Word by the preacher, too often the exposition of his subjective opinions." [9] The "response of the congregation" is vestigially present only at the offering and intercessions on most Sundays. If such vestige is not sufficient reminder of the central act, we have no place to go but to the weekly celebration of the sacrament of Holy Communion. Even then the problem for us is not simple. The sacramental practice, too, has degenerated into a subjective sentimentality. The hymns used are damning evidence of this, as are phrases like "come not because you must but because you may."

The laymen, therefore, have discovered an identical problem in both Word and sacrament. They say that we must relinquish the pretension to having the initiative in any sense whatsoever. In both Word and sacrament the initiative is God's. In other words, life is sacramental, and whether it be through speaking and hearing or through acting out, we are to be exposed to a dramatic reminder of the life, death, resurrection, glorious ascension, and eternal habitation of our Lord. P. T. Forsyth puts it this way: "It made all the difference to the religious history of the first Church that they observed a sacrament in the centre of their worship, and did not offer a sacrifice." [10] If the sacrifice was once for all, we still cannot evade the responsibility of responding to that sacrifice through an acting out of the pledge of obedience, together with the songs of praise and thanksgiving.

In this connection the same reformation has come up with a second surprise, namely that the so-called priestly functions are not to be reserved for the functioning clergy.

Any one of the company of the faithful can call the congregation to worship. If he himself is ready to confess, he may lead in the confession and share his own conviction of God's forgiveness. A member can lead in, as he shares in, the prayers of thanksgiving and dedication and in the acts of intercession. The direction in which this reform seems to be moving has some troublesome implications for the sacramental practice, but the questions remain creative. Who is the host at the table but Christ alone? Is it competence or some other qualification which permits a man to function in Christ's name in the breaking and the distribution of the bread and in the pouring and the passing of the cup? Is it, as Forsyth has suggested, the body, broken, and the blood, shed, or is it the body broken and the blood shed? In the fully shared feast does the question of administering diminish in importance? With a living presence in our reunited midst, is not the joy of the marriage feast sufficient to overcome the difficulties involved in appointing the seating arrangement?

The priestly office and function is a "central point of controversy," we can agree. But if the Roman Church can move "to introduce, at least gradually, the practice of Communion under both kinds," [11] it may be possible, at least for the Free Church, to relinquish priestly prerogatives, especially in light of the fact that for us those prerogatives do not comprise an intrinsic claim. I am assuming, of course, that other points of sharp difference, such as concelebration, are subject to reform, and that we may have a refined definition of the calling initiated by the Holy Spirit and the "ministry" acknowledged by God as well as, or even apart from, man.

The deliberations by these disciplined laymen are reducing the minister to the role of a workman. But they have the effect of increasing the responsibility to be the good "workman who has no need to be ashamed" (2 Tim. 2:15b). The minister is one person among the gathered people in competition with all the rest of them, as it were, in "showing zeal" and otherwise exhibiting the fruits of the Spirit. He is called upon to be at least as effective in his workshop as the engineer and architect are in theirs, so that when the troops regather on a Sunday to report the success and failure of the week, all will have taken the risk of holy witness, suffered its pain, and known its joy. Those who feel called to such a ministry may well find it plausible to accept the lay vocation with joy and thanksgiving. To proclaim "the priesthood of all believers" would seem to imply a willingness, even an eagerness, to become engaged in the general priesthood. The desire for priestly prerogatives is hardly becoming when found in those who seem to scorn the prerogatives. The tendency to want to be set apart is unseemly when found in those who say they are committed to being bound "in one living tether, the priest, the prince, the thrall." [12]

When one goes to a large corporation armed only with an address, a floor, and a name, he finds himself able to relate to the stranger with whom he has the appointment, because he has confidence in the standing of the corporation. The reputation of the corporation has been secured and established by the steady professional competence of its officers through many years. There is, of course, need for great professional competence. The Free Church position on the priesthood makes it mandatory that we move to greater competence for the whole priesthood as steadily and speedily as possible. However, once the standing of a particular company of the faithful people is established, I doubt that titles and other prerogatives will loom any larger in importance in the Church than they do to the outsider walking up and down the long corridors of a huge corporation.

From the point of view of the Free Church tradition, the priesthood of all believers must begin to live and breathe in some of these dimensions, or else it must be discarded as an

unworthy slogan which was born in a bitter day and is irrelevant to the rapid changes of today.

Conclusion

It is salutary that these principles are now being exposed
to critical scrutiny by Vatican as well as World Council
ecumenists, Christians who care profoundly for the reconciled and reconciling community and are increasingly reckless about any criteria except gospel and Holy Spirit. After
a few years together in the United Church of Christ, there
will be need for further scrutiny to see whether we have
grasped the expanded theological opportunity or lapsed in-
differently into a theological neutralism, to see whether we
have achieved a coalescence of polities or a mutual accommodation of the unfaithful weaknesses in each. We beseech
your prayers.

In the meantime, the United Church seems committed
to the Church evangelical and catholic, and further committed to any indicated and significant sacrifice of denominational identity. For these commitments we are profoundly
grateful and hopeful.

The reason for our hope is something more radical than
the increase of a general good will and mutual understanding.
We look to the structural realization of the unity of Christ's
Church, not now or ever to be disestablished. Dr. Tillich
writes: "The Protestant principle . . . not restricted to the
churches of the Reformation . . . [is] an expression of the
Spiritual Community. . . . It alone is not enough; it needs
the 'Catholic substance,' the concrete embodiment of the
Spiritual Presence. . . ." [13]

Many of us in the United Church of Christ pray that this
communion may be useful to any development holding promise for a creative and continuing tension between the "Protestant principle" and the "Catholic substance."

4

William H. Lazareth:

The Future of American Lutheranism

"Lutheran theology is 90 per cent cross and 10 per cent crass," complained one friendly but exasperated colleague after a heated discussion at the 1963 Faith and Order Conference in Montreal. There is probably some truth in this fraternal barb. It points to that peculiar quality which many non-Lutherans find at once admirable and deplorable in the ecumenical stance of evangelical Lutheranism. At worst this posture reflects little more than the stubbornness of doctrinal pride. At best, however, it expresses the tenacity of Christians in witnessing to their understanding of the "faith which was once for all delivered to the saints."

1

The distinctive approach of Lutherans to the Christian Church is marked by both reverence and freedom: reverence because Christ is there, freedom because much that is not Christ is also there. Lutherans revere the Church because they cannot separate it from Christ. Yet they also feel free to re-

form the Church because they do not identify it with Christ.
People who shake their heads in dismay when Lutheran theology describes Christians as "at once righteous and sinful,"
are only further confounded when the Christian Church is
likewise designated as "at once holy and sinful."

It should therefore be said at the outset that no Lutheran
worth his salt could ever have more than a "lover's quarrel"
with the Church. Current talk of a Christian "no-Church
movement," for example, strikes him as bordering on blas-
phemy. This is because Lutherans believe that the Church
and its means of grace are the creation and gifts of God's Holy
Spirit. Only in the Church do men find the forgiveness of
sin, and life, and salvation. It would therefore be impossible
for Lutherans to separate faithful discipleship from responsible churchmanship.

When some sixteenth-century radicals confused their
brand of the "no-Church movement" with Christian liberty,
Luther was the first to insist on the corporate nature of the
people of God. He preached:

Any one who is to find Christ must first find the Church. For
how can one know where Christ is, and where faith in him is,
unless he knew where his believers are? Whoever wishes to
know something about Christ must not trust to himself, nor by
the help of his own reason build a bridge of his own to heaven,
but must go to the church, must visit it, and make inquiry. Now
the Church is not wood and stone, but the company of the people who believe in Christ. He must keep in company with them
and see how they believe, and teach, and live. (*WA* 10, I, 1
140)

At the same time, the Lutheran's priestly "yes" to the
Church is always balanced by a prophetic "no." It is the
special calling of those who have been trained in Christian
theology to hold the Church's faith and order accountable

to God's sovereign Word, the proclamation of the gospel. The Christian Church, sinful as well as holy, is in need of continual self-examination and reformation. It remains the Church of Christ because, and only in so far as, it remains faithful to the gospel of God's self-revelation.

This was the burning conviction that compelled Luther to lead a reform within the Church rather than a revolt against it. He wrote:

The Church is engendered through the Word. Therefore you must say that the Church is less than the Word. Why, then, do you say that the Church is superior to the Word? It is the same as saying that the child is superior to the mother. But, on the contrary, it is the mother who bears and nurtures the child. Christianity is a child, pure and simple, a mere babe apart from the Word. She is judged and guided by the Word. Therefore she cannot judge the Word of God; if she does, she is a harlot, not a mother. (*WA* 17, I, 99)

In short, Lutherans confess that the Church of Jesus Christ is at once the daughter of the proclaimed Word of God and the mother of the redeemed children of God. This is the paradoxical ecclesiology which is at the heart of the often misunderstood commitment of evangelical Lutheranism to ecumenical Christianity.

On the one hand, supporters of the Ecumenical Movement have often been attacked for sacrificing Christian truth to manifest more church unity. On the other hand, opponents of the Ecumenical Movement have likewise been criticized for sabotaging church unity for the sake of their version of the Christian truth. As supporters of some ecumenical activities and opponents of others, Lutherans have consistently pleaded that Christian truth and unity both serve the Church's primary mission: "that the world may believe."

Hence Lutherans now face a peculiar challenge as they

try to "speak the truth in love" with Christian brothers in other churches. To pose the dilemma as boldly as possible: As members of a church which believes that it certainly—though not exclusively—confesses the one true faith in Jesus Christ, can Lutherans avoid the twin pitfalls of sterile isolationism and sentimental unionism? Can divided churchmen in a pluralistic culture be at once evangelical and ecumenical in their faithful witness to the one Lord of the one Church?

Perhaps we might more fully appreciate the tension involved here by recalling the two opposite ways in which Peter betrayed his Lord. Strange as it seems, Peter first betrayed Christ by denying his accent. Then he later betrayed Christ by overstressing it.

We remember that just before the crucifixion, Peter was called on by Christ's enemies to witness to his Master. But he was alone and frightened. The power of the Holy Spirit was not yet within him. When challenged to confess Christ, he could only cry out in despair, "I do not know the man!"

Then the Gospel of Matthew records an ironic twist: "After a little while the bystanders came up and said to Peter, 'Certainly you are also one of them, for your accent betrays you'" (26:73). The Jerusalem "city slickers" knew that "he was one of them" because they could always tell a "hick" from the country when they heard one. The strange fact is that Peter betrayed Christ by betraying his own Galilean accent. "Then he began to invoke a curse on himself and to swear, 'I do not know the man'" (26:74). In other words, the more Peter denied his accent, the more Peter denied his Lord.

Paradoxically it was this same apostle who later betrayed Christ by overstressing his accent. This time, however, it was his theological accent which was at the root of his trouble. In the second chapter of Galatians, we hear Paul complaining about Peter's denial of Christian liberty by resorting to Jewish legalism when it came to eating with Gentiles:

But when Cephas came to Antioch I opposed him to his face, because he stood condemned. For before certain men came from James, he ate with the Gentiles; but when they came he drew back and separated himself, fearing the circumcision party. . . . But when I saw that they were not straightforward about the gospel, I said to Cephas before them all. . . . "We know that a man is not justified by works of the law but through faith in Jesus Christ!" (2:11-16)

Speaking symbolically, Peter's experiences should help to illumine the two dangers which Lutherans must try to avoid in witnessing to Jesus Christ in an ecumenical age. Whether they like it or not, every one of them has learned to speak the Christian language with a strong Lutheran accent. And, like Peter, they suffer perennial temptations either to deny it or to revel in it.

It is often as difficult for Christians to relate the universal to the particular in Christ's Body as in the Church's head. As God was incarnate in the man Jesus, the kingdom of God is now present in local congregations and even separate denominations. This means that weak men can become Arians or Docetists in their ecclesiology as well as in their Christology.

For example, a Lutheran Christian is baptized as an infant into the one, holy, catholic, and apostolic Church. He is then confirmed a few years later as a communing member of St. Paul's Evangelical Lutheran Church of the Rochester District of the New York Synod of the Lutheran Church in America. During every church year, he shares in the painful privilege of celebrating Reformation Day and All Saints' Day side by side, back to back. In this ambiguous situation, he can easily rend asunder "that which God hath joined together." Men are continually tempted either to defy or to deify the peculiar gifts which the Lord of the Church has granted to those of his disciples who now call themselves "evangelical Lutherans."

II

What are the distinctive marks of Lutheran Christianity? Generalizations are always hazardous, because of the exceptions they overlook. Sweeping assertions are usually unfair to someone. Nevertheless, Holy Scripture admonishes us to try to read the "handwriting on the wall" and perceive the "signs of the times." It should go without saying that no Lutheran essayist speaks as an official representative of his church when it comes to such corporate self-examination. Personally, however, I believe that Lutheranism has three outstanding characteristics. In terms of both evangelical depth and catholic breadth, Lutherans at best have been pastoral, confessional, and liturgical.

In the first place, the Lutheran Church has had a *pastoral* concern for the individual soul. It has always been ready to proclaim God's law and gospel in order to grant disobedient and troubled men Christ's pardon for their sin and the Spirit's power for their renewal. A strong ministry of serving love has also resulted in hundreds of homes, agencies, and institutions in which Christian compassion is shown to the weak, the old, the sick, and the oppressed. It is probably no accident that Lutherans prefer to call their clergy "pastor," or that there is no real equivalent in English for *Seelsorge*. This pastoral "care of souls" is a characteristic feature of the conscientious Lutheran minister. He has a personal concern for each individual sheep whom he has been called by God to shepherd into eternal life.

In this connection, it should be underscored that nothing is more revealing of the Lutheran spirit than the importance it attaches to the proclamation of the gospel (*viva vox evangelii*). The pastor's authority is grounded solely in his office, which in turn derives its authority from the gospel message. Since "faith comes from what is heard," the ordained minis-

try is viewed as a functional office—not a sacerdotal order—
which is bound to proclaim God's Word in speech and in
action. As evangelical Christians, Lutherans attribute the
church's final authority to the Christ of the Bible—the living
Word of God—and they confess that this Word is effectively
communicated to men by preaching and the administration of
baptism and the Lord's Supper. In the judgment of Wilhelm
Pauck:

Only the new understanding of the gospel achieved by Luther
and his fellow Reformers led to such an emphasis upon the proclamation of the Word that henceforth the very reality of the
church was grounded in preaching. The seventh article of the
Augsburg Confession, in which Melanchthon summarized the
faith of the Lutherans for presentation at the Diet of Augsburg
in 1530, defined the church as 'the congregation of the saints in
which the gospel is rightly preached and the sacraments are
rightly administered.' [1]

Second, Lutheran theology has been soundly *confessional*
in proclaiming Jesus Christ as Lord. As the mother church
of the Reformation, Lutherans have always been called on to
justify the "tragic necessity" of that great restoration of evangelical faith and life to the rest of the corrupted Body of
Christ. More recently, Lutherans have also had to disassociate
themselves from those periodic outbursts of sentimental relig-
iosity which likewise bear so little resemblance to the scriptural Word of God. The multitude of so-called "Protestant"
sects and cults in the United States demonstrates clearly that
man's religion remains the chief enemy of God's revelation.
Confessional theology, firmly centered in the good news of
the New Testament, has been a hallmark of the Lutheran
evangelical tradition.

This Christ-centered faith is evident throughout the confessions (creedal documents) of the Lutheran Church. Along
with the three ancient creeds, the *Book of Concord* (1580)

includes the following six works which develop the Lutheran position on the major theological controversies that divided the Christian Church in the sixteenth century: the *Small Catechism* and the *Large Catechism* (1529) were written as doctrinal guides for the instruction of youth and the preaching of pastors. The *Augsburg Confession* (1530), *Apology of the Augsburg Confession* (1531), and *Smalcald Articles* (1537) explain the biblical foundations of Lutheran doctrine, and also contrast its teachings with the beliefs of Roman Catholics and those of other Protestants. The *Formula of Concord* (1577) helped to settle doctrinal disputes among Lutherans after the death of the Reformer. All these confessions witness to the central authority of the Word of God mediated by the Spirit through the Holy Scriptures.

Finally, the Lutheran Church has been *liturgical* in its sensitivity to good order and reverence in its adoration of the living God. The church's conservative reformation was concerned with eliminating only those objectionable features of the Roman mass which belied the Christ-centered character of authentic Christian worship. All other churchly ceremonies, symbols, and appointments which serve faith as channels of the gospel were gladly kept and treasured as worthy means to praise God's holy name. Whether simple or elaborate, the church's liturgy has been gratefully respected by the worshiping community. In the words of Luther D. Reed:

The genius of Lutheranism reacts not only against a casual or irreverent approach to God, but also against externality and display in public worship. We seek to approach God directly, simply, sincerely. The simplicity and forthrightness of our liturgy require corresponding qualities in its setting and rendition. Over-elaboration, fussy decoration, excessive ceremonial, concertistic music are all out of harmony with the Lutheran understanding. A strong sense of historic values and of what is inherently worshipful, distinctive, and beautiful, however, is entirely in the Lutheran spirit. . . . Worship is a means to an end. It must establish men and women in communion with God and in the fellowship of the saints.[2]

Pastoral, confessional, liturgical: these key features, I suggest, are most typical of the faith and life of Lutheran Christianity. That is the ideal Lutherans strive after, the way they hope to witness to God and men at their best. But life is lived in the actual, and not the ideal. These goals are far easier to preach than to practice. The two besetting temptations of Peter return to plague Lutherans as every generation in the church responds somewhat differently to the changing demands of its age. In the light of these three distinguishing characteristics, let us now hazard an over-all look at American Lutheranism. Where has it been, and where is it going?

III

At the expense of distorted oversimplification, I would suggest that American Lutherans in the past have usually succumbed to the temptation of the late Peter whenever they have fallen short of the ideal. That is, they often overemphasized their Lutheran accent at the expense of their evangelical catholicity.

This ecclesiastical provincialism is understandable, even if not wholly justifiable. Lutheran churches were largely immigrant churches, and they usually tried to maintain their familiar languages, customs, and way of life in their new home-away-from-home. Many of them were already dissenters from the dominant religious traditions of the established churches of their native soil. They felt doubly threatened in a new country when challenged by all kinds of strange peoples, beliefs, and practices. It was only natural that many of these German and Scandinavian Pietists gradually withdrew into the security of small, ethnically homogeneous communities. As a temporary, transitional maneuver, this defensive stance had much to commend it. Its indefinite perpetuation, however, exacted a heavy toll on American Lutheranism's "characteristic" (but un-Lutheran!) way of life.

First, pastoral care for the person often degenerated into a kind of ecclesiastical *individualism*. There was very little concern for the church outside the walls of the local congregation. Charity not only began, but often ended, right at home. Congregations gave next to no support to synods; they in turn gave even less help to the work of the church at large. "Herr Pastor" often ruled with an iron hand as the undisputed leader of his own little personality cult. If a congregation did not like a particular action or program of the synod, it simply quit. The novelty of "congregational autonomy" was uncritically absorbed from the new religious culture, as cell after cell of unaffiliated Lutherans practiced a policy of "live and let live," and even "die and let die."

At the same time, the Lutheran confessional concern, when confronted with all kinds of liberal teachings and unevangelical sects, often hardened into a very unlovely type of *dogmatism*. Faith in God became virtually identical with beliefs about God. A rock-ribbed biblicism became far more interested in exposing how Lutherans differed from Calvinists and Roman Catholics than in revealing how they compared with Jesus Christ. A rigid scholasticism led some Lutherans to deny pulpit and altar fellowship to some of their less narrow fellow confessionalists. A legalistic moralism prompted the cutting of still more ties with brothers in Christ over minor disputes on adiaphoral matters which the church had formerly left to Christian freedom.

There is a note of irony in this whole development. Lutherans have been blessed with a strong evangelical tradition which staunchly refuses to allow man to take any credit for earning his salvation. To Christ, they humbly confess, belongs all the glory. But this very humility—especially when contrasted with more Pelagian theologies—becomes something that sinful men can then take pride in! In fact, Lutherans have sometimes taken pride in being "not like those other men" who do take pride in working out their own salvation. Despite all their theological erudition, Lutherans were often unaware that this is about as sophisticated a form of intellectual work-righteousness as you can get.

Finally, the Lutheran liturgy, particularly in foreign languages, often contributed to their cultic and communal *isolationism*. "Lutherians" or "Lutheranians" were generally characterized by their neighbors as clean, honest, hard-working "rugged individualists." They seldom bothered anybody else, and they expected the same privacy in return. As foreigners, Lutherans were often looked upon with suspicion, especially since their doctrinal position apparently forbade them to engage in very much common worship or work with fellow Christians. Indeed, Protestants of the Free Church tradition generally considered Lutherans to be "half-Catholic," because of their formal liturgical worship and general distrust of religious revivalism and moral crusades. In short, liturgy also helped to erect and perpetuate the barriers between Lutherans and the Puritanical and revivalistic religious culture in the United States.

How blighting a combination this individualism, dogmatism, and isolationism could prove to be was vividly illustrated some years ago, when an old German Lutheran congregation was suddenly faced with an influx of Puerto Ricans in their community. The synod encouraged them to minister to the whole neighborhood. They pleaded with them not to perpetuate the Teutonic alumni association which they were operating. After much debate, the church council decided that they would meet the problem head on. They magnanimously set aside an afternoon a week when all Spanish-speaking persons in the community would be offered free language lessons. But in order to help any prospective members to memorize the liturgy and Luther's catechism, all the lessons were naturally to be held *auf Deutsch!*

It comes as no surprise, therefore, to find this American Lutheran insularity being publicly deplored in the non-denominational *Christian Century* as late as 1940. Editor Harold E. Fey lamented:

In the [recent] rediscovery by American Protestantism of the truth and the faith through which the Reformation brought new spiritual life to Western Christianity, Lutherans of America would do well to weigh the fact that they have played an almost negligible role. Their policy of isolation has debarred them from impregnating the rest of Protestantism with the very truths which it has lost and which Lutheranism possesses. . . . But the Lutheran churches at the very moment in history when the mind of Protestantism is open as never before to what they have to give, have so insulated themselves that the vital contact or channel through which their witness could be made effective is practically non-existent. (Oct. 23, 1940, p. 1324)

Lutherans might rightly protest that such a blanket charge was highly unfair. It did not take into account either the deplorable state of Protestant liberalism or the formidable obstacles faced by the immigrant Lutheran churches. Moreover, there are some notable exceptions, and even contradictions, to the very rough historical sketch which we have drawn. These would include the wide influence of Wilhelm Loehe's non-congregational polity, S. S. Schmucker's non-confessional theology, and Ole Hallesby's non-liturgical piety.

Nevertheless, to the eyes of most non-Lutheran observers in the past, the "little oaks of Saxony" in America appeared to succumb most often to the temptation of the late Peter in overstressing their Lutheran accent at the expense of their evangelical catholicity.

IV

Some time during the turn of the mid-century, the slumbering bear of American Lutheranism finally emerged from its cultural and ecclesiastical hibernation. External influences included the welcome development of a more conservative religious climate in U.S. Protestantism, along with the crying need for a co-ordinated response to the desperate plight of the victims of World War II. At the same time, internal changes began to take place rapidly as acculturated ex-immigrants responded loyally and sacrificially to dynamic new church leadership.

Symptomatic of this revolution was a 1958 cover story which *Time* magazine devoted to the Lutheran pastor who did the most to make it possible, Dr. Franklin Clark Fry. The cover portrait captured him proclaiming the gospel; a second illustration showed him receiving Holy Communion. On this evangelical foundation, the feature lauded the ecumenical churchmanship of "perhaps the most influential leader of world Protestantism."

Time's secular judgment—appearing less than twenty years after the indictment of the *Christian Century*—is especially noteworthy: "Of all the denominations in the United States, Lutheranism is experiencing the most dramatic new birth, and Franklin Clark Fry, more than any other Lutheran, is its symbol. . . . Today, while still strongly tradition-bound, U.S. Lutheranism is emerging from isolation" (April 7, 1958, p. 58).

In this entirely new setting, American Lutherans may now be much more prone to surrender to the temptation of the early Peter: namely, to deny their distinctive accent in order to insure their public acceptance. "Arriving on Main Street" has already proved costly in various quarters of the church. In a futile attempt to compensate for past short-comings, some minority pockets of Lutherans have become possessed with a burning desire to become "Americanized" and "Protestantized" as quickly as possible. This has resulted in the present dilemma: How "successful" can a church become and still remain the self-sacrificing Body of a crucified Lord? May not a church so conform to the world that the salt will lose its flavor and the leaven its power?

In church polity, there are signs that some Lutherans want to move from their old individualism to a new *collectivism*. Their political approach to Christian ecumenism is often based on little more than a fear of Roman Catholicism.

In church theology, there are signs that some Lutherans want to move from their old dogmatism to a new *relativism*. Their cavalier approach to Christian doctrine is usually rooted in nothing more than an addiction to ecclesiastical activism.

In church worship, there are signs that some Lutherans want to move from their old isolation to a new *assimilation*. Their aesthetic approach to Christian liturgy generally results in pitting "high" and "low" church practices over against each other in arid competition.

We must reject all these false alternatives as secularistic threats to the reconciling mission of the church. Instead we will explore some of the ways by which American Lutherans might better express their evangelical depth and catholic breadth in future relations with (1) their fellow Lutherans, (2) their non-Lutheran fellow Christians, and (3) their non-Christian fellow men.

V

Turning first to the thorny problem of Lutheran unity, it would be well to remember that of the world's seventy million Lutherans, some nine million are centered in three major churches of roughly like size in the United States. The Lutheran Church in America was formed in 1962 as a result of the merger of the American Evangelical Lutheran Church (of Danish origin), the Augustana Evangelical Lutheran Church (of Swedish origin), the Finnish Evangelical Lutheran Church of America (Suomi Synod), and the United Lutheran Church in America (mainly of German origin). The American Lutheran Church was created in 1960 on the basis of a merger of the American Lutheran Church (of German origin), the Evangelical Lutheran Church (of Norwegian origin), and the United Evangelical Lutheran Church (of Danish origin). Side by side with these two churches is a third chief body, the Lutheran Church–Missouri Synod (of German origin).

The National Lutheran Council has served since 1918 as the focal point for most of the broad interchurch co-operation among America's Lutherans. Heretofore, however, the Lutheran Church–Missouri Synod has not found it possible to become an official member of any such co-operative agency. Happily, that time seems to be past, especially since the restricting ties that bound Missouri Lutherans with the ultra-orthodox Joint Synod of Wisconsin (350,000 members) have now been severed.*

Plans are now under way which call for the establishment in 1967 of a new agency, the membership of which will include almost all U.S. Lutherans. The functions of this new "Lutheran Council in the U.S.A." are to include the-

* As a welcome harbinger of future ecumenical developments, we might cite a 1963 study document prepared by Missouri's official Commission on Theology and Church Relations. It offers a biblical but clearly non-scholastic alternative to Missouri's traditional approach to revelation, inspiration, and the inerrancy of Holy Scripture. If widely accepted this viewpoint could be of great help in liberating the Missouri Synod to strengthen its ties with other evangelical church bodies. Copies are available from the Concordia Publishing House, 3558 South Jefferson Avenue, St. Louis, Missouri.

ological study, missions, education, social welfare, public
relations, service to military personnel, and other special
activities. The preamble of its constitution states that member churches will work together in "matters of common interest and responsibility, co-operation in which is not at
variance with their doctrine and practice." It states the traditional Lutheran basis of doctrine for member churches—
that they "acknowledge the Holy Scriptures of the Old and
New Testaments as the only source and infallible norm of all
church doctrine and practice." It adds that member churches
"see in the ecumenical creeds and confessions of the Lutheran
church, especially in the Unaltered Augsburg Confession and
Luther's Small Catechism, a pure exposition of the Word of
God."

For most American Protestants, that much doctrinal
agreement would be more than enough for organic union.
(It would also satisfy most European Lutherans.) But for
American Lutherans, it is barely adequate for the formation
of a co-operative agency. Apparently it is not enough even
to serve as the foundation for common pulpit and altar fellowship among the prospective member churches. Consequently in January, 1964, the American Lutheran Church and
the Lutheran Church–Missouri Synod inaugurated a parallel
set of theological negotiations to determine whether such
fraternal fellowship between them as brother Lutherans ought
to be sanctioned.

The Lutheran Church in America has not chosen to enter into these discussions, although it continues to pledge
that "our arms are open wide to our brethren." Many churchmen have been puzzled by this stance taken by the most ecumenically minded Lutheran body in America. Because of the
crucial importance of this issue for the future of American
Lutheran unity, we have received permission to quote at some
length from the official explanation issued by President Fry
in March, 1964. It reads:

The main fact is that, to my gratification and I am sure to yours, our Lutheran Church in America has already, on its part, extended full church fellowship to both of the bodies which have decided to engage in new conversations. Nothing more exists that we can give. The Confession of Faith in our own LCA constitution declares for all the world to read in one of its noblest passages: 'this church accepts the Unaltered Augsburg Confession and Luther's Small Catechism as true witnesses to the gospel, *and acknowledges as one with it in faith and doctrine all churches that likewise accept the teachings of these symbols*' (italics added).

Any negotiations for us, having said that, would be a strange, one-legged affair.

Furthermore, this theological stance of the Lutheran Church in America corresponds precisely to the one endorsed by the Lutheran World Federation by a ringing vote, accompanied by vigorous applause, at Helsinki last summer [1963]. It shows our loyalty to, and our identification with, the convictions of the overwhelming majority of the whole Lutheran family on earth. This is what the Assembly meant when it charged the incoming executive committee to 'ascertain which member churches find themselves unable to *declare* pulpit and altar fellowship with other member churches of the LWF, ask them to indicate their reasons for this position, and urge them to enter into fraternal theological discussion *concerning these reasons.*' That shifts the burden of proof completely around.

Underlying the LCA position is the conviction that, for purposes of polity, a Lutheran church can be identified as one which holds the Christian faith in accord with the confessional writings of the Lutheran Church. On the vexing issue of church unity, Articles IV and VII of the Augsburg Confession are clear and unequivocal in defining what alone is essential. Article IV declares that the heart of the proclamation of the gospel is that "men cannot be justified before God by their own strength, merits, or works, but are freely justified for Christ's sake, through faith." The same confession then goes on to affirm that it is this gospel alone which unites Christ's Church in purity and in truth. Article VII reads:

It is also taught among us that one holy Christian Church will be and remain forever. This is the assembly of all believers among whom the gospel is preached in its purity and the holy sacraments are administered according to the gospel. For it is sufficient for the true unity of the Christian Church that the gospel be preached in conformity with a pure understanding of it and that the sacraments be administered in accordance with the divine Word. It is not necessary for the true unity of the Christian Church that ceremonies, instituted by men, should be observed uniformly in all places (Eph. 4:4-5).[3]

In a forthright essay on the implications of these articles for Lutheran unity in America, Dr. Conrad Bergendoff has charged, "When unity of faith already exists, it is merely to confuse the issue to introduce the discussion of doctrine when only the question of organization is involved." In other words, it is actually an implicit rejection of the Lutheran confessions when modern American Lutherans attempt to add to what the confessions themselves declare "is enough" (*satis est*) for manifesting church unity. It is as anticonfessional for Lutherans to demand too much as it is to permit too little when it comes to qualifications for church fellowship among brothers in the gospel. Concludes Dr. Bergendoff:

When therefore we speak of Lutheran unity, we mean that unity which centers in a common faith in the Christ of Word and sacrament. Where that faith exists, there is a unity whether we recognize it or not. But I cannot see how we can refuse to recognize it where it is declared. Every Lutheran synod, or church, in America professes that common faith, and bases its profession on the same confessions. We ought to thank God for this unity and express our faith and love by acknowledging each other as Lutherans.

The test of Lutheran unity is the declaration of each body as to its doctrine of the gospel and the sacraments, and where there is this agreement, it is *enough* for Lutheran fellowship. Those are not true to the confessions who will require more than this. To build up new confessional statements 'in miniature' or to add new stipulations for unity is going beyond the confessions of the Lutheran Church and introducing division rather than unity in the church.[4]

Who is a "real" Lutheran? is therefore the ludicrous question that has yet to be resolved before any breakthrough can occur in either pulpit and altar fellowship or eventual organic merger among the major Lutheran bodies in America. Any future reforms in American Lutheran polity will certainly have to take the following factors into consideration:

First, it may confidently be asserted that persisting American Lutheran divisions are due far less to living differences in evangelical doctrine than to dead (or rapidly dying) differences in language, culture, and geography.

Second, it is therefore difficult to escape the ecumenical conclusion that persisting American Lutheran divisions are among those unnecessary breaches within the one Church of Christ which are a *scandalon* to its unity and mission.

Third, it may well be that Lutheran unity will not appreciably antedate other vital expressions of Christian unity, but will rather come about eventually as still another of the by-products which are "added unto" those followers of Christ who faithfully seek first the kingdom of God and his righteousness.

Turning next to the formidable area of *Lutheran doctrine*, we might begin by recalling one of the embarrassing headlines with which the secular press caricatured the theological debates at Helsinki's 1963 Assembly of the Lutheran World Federation: "Lutherans Can't Justify Justification."

Actually no voices were raised questioning *whether* the redemptive reality described by the doctrine of justification by grace through faith is really at the heart of the Christian faith. What was asked endlessly, however, was *how* this message must now be proclaimed to modern man in order to bear faithful witness to the same unchanging redemptive reality. In the words of the Assembly message:

The man of today no longer asks, 'How can I find a gracious God?' His question is more radical, more elementary: he asks about God as such, 'Where is God?' He suffers, not from God's wrath, but from the impression of his absence; not from sin, but from the meaninglessness of his existence; he asks, not about a gracious God, but whether God really exists. . . .

'Jesus Christ, the same yesterday, today, and forever'—this means, not that we are curators of a museum of ecclesiastical antiquities, but that we bear witness to the presence of God through Christ in our midst today. It does not mean that we want to surrender the answer which our fathers gave to the question concerning the gracious God—this has been the intention of no one at this great gathering of Lutheran churches; but we are rather to give this answer anew in our generation, so that it may remain the same answer.[5]

Here in a nutshell the Assembly revealed the point of greatest need in reforming Lutheran doctrine: "Particular theologies . . . have sprung out of specific historical situations and are involved in the rise and fall of history. . . . We are therefore summoned to a fearless and honest encounter with contemporary thought." In other words, after centuries of speaking almost exclusively with each other, twentieth-century Lutherans have finally been compelled to admit the truth of Reinhold Niebuhr's epigram: "Nothing is quite so incredible as an answer to an unasked question."

This is not a problem peculiar to Lutherans; all Christian churches are wrestling today with the need to pour the wine of the gospel into new cultural wineskins. Yet European Lutherans have been particularly creative in their exploratory attempts to reform the theological heritage of Luther and Lutheranism in order to address the plight of modern man. One thinks immediately of such a variegated company of theologians as Aulen, Nygren, and Wingren of Sweden; Prenter and Skydsgaard of Denmark; and Bonhoeffer, Bultmann, Tillich, Ebeling, and Thielicke of Germany.

It goes without saying that very few American Lutheran theologians have reached this stature. Again, this is an acute problem shared by most Protestant churches in the United States. During the past century, "activistic" pastors in mission churches had little time for writing theology when there were frontiers to convert or boatloads of immigrants to care for. "Deeds, not creeds" became the hallmark of American Protestantism. But that situation is now changing. First-rate theology is beginning to be written by Protestants in this country. By and large, it is emanating from the strong non-denominational seminaries (recently including some Lutheran faculty members) which are related to top-grade universities in our urban centers.

If American Lutherans are to make an ecumenical contribution which is in any way commensurate with their rich theological tradition, it is our conviction that they must rapidly merge their limited and scattered resources into fewer, stronger seminaries which are likewise urban-oriented and university-related. Of course, such a strategy could not of itself guarantee the desired "fearless and honest encounter with contemporary thought," but it would certainly make its present avoidance a lot more difficult.*

---

* By way of practical implementation, this position has already been developed by the author in support of a proposed merger of the two Lutheran seminaries now at Philadelphia and Gettysburg, with relocation in the urban renewal project surrounding the University of Pennsylvania. *Cf.* "Seminary Report," *Minutes of the Second Convention of the New York Synod of the Lutheran Church in America, 1963,* p. 103-104.

During the past century it was right and proper for weak, divided churches in a new land, in the midst of conflicting faiths, to preserve the Lutheran understanding of the gospel in a number of small and isolated institutions throughout the land. Faced by tremendous obstacles, their over-all accomplishments were often heroic. But the combined resources of newly merged churches should now make it possible for Lutheran practice to disavow the American sectarian pattern of divorcing the "sacred" from the "secular." Despite all the disadvantages of a late arrival, it is now imperative that Lutherans reassume (with necessary structural modifications) the traditional theological pattern in Germany and Scandinavia. There it is simply taken for granted that the "salt" and "light" of evangelical theology is to be taught, learned, attacked, and defended within the universal context of man's total quest for truth in the midst of all the principalities and powers of the university world.

Three reasons can be outlined briefly for setting new sights in this direction: (1) theological integrity, (2) pastoral effectiveness, and (3) academic excellence.

The primary concern for theological integrity should compel Lutherans to look in the direction of a university environment and affiliation. For evangelical Christians, the task of theology is to address God's eternal Word to God's contemporary world. It is not enough for American theologians to limit themselves to translating and interpreting the works of their university-involved European colleagues. The development of an indigenous American Lutheran theology within an ecumenical Christian context could best be fostered by involving professors and students in a setting where an ongoing conversation with men of other faiths (and even of no faith) would be a stimulating part of everyday seminary life.

The benefits to students in their pastoral effectiveness

should also be obvious. The days are past when American Lutheran churches could be identified as the foreign "ghettos" of Nordic immigrants. Lutheran churches are now among the most urban Protestant bodies in the country. Pastors-to-be could best be prepared to minister to men of all ethnic and national backgrounds by learning to know and love them through personal contacts. Seminarians who know whom they are to address, as well as what they are to say, will be those most able to equip the whole people of God for their ministry to the urban, cosmopolitan world in which we increasingly find ourselves.

Such a university affiliation could not but raise the academic standards of Lutheran professors and students. Through them it would elevate the educational program of the whole church. The rapidly rising educational level of laymen, to say nothing of the increasing demands of biblical and theological scholarship, makes first-rate seminaries connected with first-rate universities an ecclesiastical necessity. This is true not only on the B.D. level. Projected plans for expanding Lutheran theological work on the graduate level could also be achieved best in a graduate-school setting which would demand academic excellence of the highest order. Then, and only then, would Lutherans be fully equipped to make a worthy ecumenical contribution to the theological life of American Christianity as a whole.

These views are not flights of fancy; they represent hard facts which Lutherans must face quickly in reforming their theological future. But the problems and costs are obviously of such magnitude that no one Lutheran body is strong enough to meet them alone. Once again, we are faced with the interrelation of the church's unity and mission. In a recent study aimed at raising theological standards and consolidating theological forces in the Lutheran Church in America, Dr. Conrad Bergendoff documented his claim that

Lutherans still "look to our seminaries to rationalize and justify our divisions." One highlight of his report:

Our reading of church history indicates that each denomination and each group within a denomination sets up its seminary to guard the boundaries which separate it from other Christians. It is the conclusion of this observer that theological education in the Lutheran Church in North America at this juncture should transcend present divisions and not be allowed to aim at perpetuation of these divisions. . . . We should plan our program on the supposition that there will be no great difference between the seminaries of the LCA and those of the ALC and the Missouri Synod. Fundamentally the theology of all Lutheran seminaries in this country is the same, and there are no theological differences that justify the multiplicity of theological schools.[6]

The ecumenical consequences of theological reform are certainly not limited to the inter-Lutheran horizon. Since Lutherans regard agreement in the proclamation of the gospel and in the administration of the sacraments to be the sole prerequisites for church unity, any major theological renewal is bound to have direct ecumenical repercussions.

To cite but one outstanding example, official delegates from both traditions are now exploring "the theological relations between the Lutheran and Reformed churches to discover to what extent differences which have divided these communions in the past still constitute obstacles to mutual understanding." Meeting regularly since 1962 have been representatives of the North American Area of the World Alliance of Reformed Churches Holding the Presbyterian Order, plus representatives from the Presbyterian Church and the Christian Reformed Church, together with those of the U.S.A. National Committee of the Lutheran World Federation—the latter group being joined by representatives from the Lutheran Church–Missouri Synod. These discussions have already resulted in two valuable sets of summary statements on "Gospel, Confession, and Scripture" and "Christology and the Lord's Supper." *

These developments in the United States parallel growing ties between the Lutherans and the Reformed abroad. Theological representatives of the Church of South India and the Lutheran churches in India have drafted a common statement of faith and are now at work on a common catechism. The Lutheran churches of Sweden and Denmark have agreed on a theological basis for intercommunion with the Reformed Church of Scotland. A similar arrangement has been made between the Lutheran and Reformed churches in the Netherlands. A widely discussed report ("Arnoldshain theses") has also been issued by theologians from Lutheran, Reformed, and Union churches in Germany as a possible basis for intercommunion among their separated bodies. Clearly the Lutheran and Reformed churches throughout the world are beginning to appreciate and bear witness more fully to their common evangelical heritage in the Reformation.

Though limits in space have compelled us to concentrate on matters of faith and order, brief mention should also be made of Lutheran piety in its life and work. Here again, we ought to recall the normative view of Lutherans that the Church's unity is of vital concern because it aids the Church's mission, but only in so far as it aids that mission. The Reformers had to learn the hard way that bigness is no guarantee of goodness in the Church. Lutherans pray that God will unite his Church *in order that* he might be glorified and his needy children served.

"That the world may believe" was also the evangelical note struck by President Fry when Texas-Louisiana became

* Copies may be obtained from the National Lutheran Council, 50 Madison Avenue, New York, New York.

the deciding synod of the old United Lutheran Church in America to ratify the merger agreements for the formation of the new Lutheran Church in America. He declared, "In its whole honorable history the ULCA has never done a worthier thing than in this decision to die. Our church is going out of existence in obedience to its Lord, who wills his Church to be one, *in order to meet the spiritual needs of twentieth-century Americans more effectively*" (italics added).

As the third largest among the Protestant denominations in America, Lutherans now play a vigorous role in the religious life of the nation. Gathered together in over 17,000 congregations in fifty states, they conduct aggressive programs in church extension, missions, education, and social welfare. Recent statistics indicate that Lutherans support 32 colleges, 20 theological seminaries, and over 1,500 elementary and high schools.

In addition, some 460 health and welfare agencies and institutions are operated, staffed by over 12,000 doctors, nurses, and social workers. Some 1,600 American Lutherans are working with the native churches in Africa, New Guinea, Japan, India, Latin America, and many other locations. Over fifty million dollars have been contributed by Lutherans since 1939 for a world-wide ministry of post-war reconstruction, healing, and reconciliation. Lutheran World Relief—a cooperative material-aid agency—has also been responsible during the past twenty years for shipping over 150 million dollars worth of food, clothing, medicines, and other relief goods to victims in forty countries throughout the world.

However, if we were pressed to name the one area in which reform is most required in Lutheran piety, it would probably be the need to integrate Christian citizenship more fully into Christian discipleship. Surrounded by Roman Catholics and Protestant sectarians, American Lutherans are continually tempted to sever the altar and the marketplace, the service of God and the service of man, the "sacred" and the "secular." Renewed stress on the priesthood of all believers—the ministry of the laity to the world and in the world—is of crucial importance today for stimulating Christian involvement in such moral crises as the Negro's struggle for human dignity and racial equality.

In the New Testament, the "worship of God" (*leiturgia, latria, diakonia*) is never limited to so-called "liturgical" practices in a sacred sanctuary. The "spiritual worship" of Christians involves "presenting your bodies as a living sacrifice" to God and neighbor throughout all of life (Rom. 12 ff.). Hence a recently published study guide for Lutheran pastors and laymen on the interaction of religion and law in a pluralistic society lays particular stress on the biblical view of the sacredness of secular life as the arena of Christian service:

The words of Jesus [in John 17:15-18] help us to understand the peculiar interaction of Christian discipleship and Christian citizenship. On the one hand, 'they are not of the world.' Christians are a holy people, saints whom God calls to be citizens in Christ's eternal kingdom of faith and love. On the other hand, 'I have sent them into the world.' Christians are also a secular people, witnesses whom God calls to be citizens in Caesar's temporal kingdom of law and justice. We confess that God remains the sole Lord of Life, whether he rules men as saints through Christ and the Church or as creatures through Caesar and the state. Consequently, our chief task is to reaffirm the 'sacred secularity' of God's people as they worship, witness, and work in his world.[7]

Ecumenical charity requires that a final word be given to a discerning non-Lutheran historian of American Protestant church life. Professor Winthrop Hudson has recently posed the paradox that the past weaknesses of American Lutherans may yet turn out to be their future strengths. He writes:

The final prospect for a vigorous renewal of Protestant life and witness rests with the Lutheran churches, which had overcome much of their fragmentation by 1960 and had grouped themselves into three main bodies. All had exhibited an ability to grow during the post-World War II years, with the Lutheran Church–Missouri Synod making the greatest gains. The Lutheran churches are in the fortunate position of having been, in varying degrees, insulated from American life for a long period of time. As a result they have been less subject to the theological erosion which so largely stripped other denominations of an awareness of their community with a historic Christian tradition. Thus the resources of the Christian past have been more readily available to them, and this fact suggests that they may have an increasingly important role in a Protestant recovery.

Among the assets immediately at hand among the Lutherans are a confessional tradition, a surviving liturgical structure, and a sense of community which, however much it may be the product of cultural factors, may make it easier for them than for most Protestant denominations to recover the 'integrity of church membership' without which Protestants are ill equipped to participate effectively in the dialogue of a pluralistic society.[8]

Certainly this generous conclusion should not blind us to the fact that American Lutherans face many grave problems in an ecumenical age. They may fail; sons of reformers are often notorious delinquents themselves. And yet, God willing, their past shortcomings (if confessed!) could well turn out to be the very points of the Holy Spirit's breakthrough in their new life together.

In summary, beyond both individualism and collectivism in church polity, there lies the Lutheran emphasis on the *pastoral* care of every member of the Body of Christ. Beyond both dogmatism and relativism in church theology, there lies the Lutheran stress on the *confessional* fidelity of the communion of saints. And beyond both isolation and assimilation in church worship, there lies the Lutheran insistence on the *liturgical* integrity of the royal priesthood. The God-given resources are all there. The only question is whether we will have the courage to use them—or better, the faith to be used by them.

Luther loved to point to the wonderful experience of Peter in walking on the waters to illustrate the vast difference between *certitudo* and *securitas*. When Peter looked faithfully into the eyes of the Lord, he knew divine certainty—and in obedience he became a walking miracle. But when he looked down to his feet in the vain quest for human security—then in disobedience he began to sink. American Lutherans face an ecumenical future with the same two alternatives: a warm heart or cold feet. *Veni Creator Spiritus!*

5

Colin W. Williams:

On Being Free for Christ's Work in the World

In February, 1739, George Whitefield, a young priest of the Church of England, found himself excluded from preaching in the churches of Bristol. But finding also that the coalminers were as eager to hear as their betters were to exclude, he resorted to preaching in the open air. To his astonishment, he soon found himself preaching to thousands; and the mounting interest forced him to look for someone to carry on the work when he left to fulfill appointments in America. The call was sent to another young Anglican priest, working with Religious Societies in London—John Wesley.

The invitation to Wesley met with resistance. He was disinclined to accede to the request. Preaching outside to the masses, in disregard of parish boundaries and without regular ecclesiastical authorization, smacked too much of a schismatic spirit. His brother Charles was "extremely averse," being a strict churchman constantly on guard against the dangers of dissent. Yet both were driven to agree that John had no

22717

choice but to obey the urgent appeal as a direct call from God. His *Journal* entries tell the story of the tense struggle against precedent, and the decision that the new demands of mission called for the acceptance of "responsible risk." *

Sat. 31 (March 1739)—In the evening I reached Bristol, and met Mr. Whitefield there. I could scarce reconcile myself at first to this strange way of preaching in the fields, of which he set me an example on Sunday; having been all my life (till very lately) so tenacious of every point relating to decency and order, that I should have thought the saving of souls almost a sin if it had not been done in a church.

April 1, Sun.—In the evening, Mr. Whitefield being gone, I began expounding our Lord's Sermon on the Mount (one pretty remarkable precedent of field-preaching, though I suppose there were churches at that time also) to a little society which was accustomed to meet once or twice a week in Nicholas Street.

Mon. 2—At four in the afternoon I submitted to be more vile, and proclaimed in the highways the glad tidings of salvation, speaking from a little eminence in a ground adjoining to the city, to about three thousand people. The Scripture on which I spoke was this (is it possible anyone should be ignorant that it is fulfilled in every true minister of Christ?), 'The Spirit of the Lord is upon me, because He hath anointed Me to preach the gospel to the poor. He hath sent Me to heal the broken-hearted; to preach deliverance to the captives, and recovery of sight to the blind; to set at liberty them that are bruised, to proclaim the acceptable year of the Lord.' [1]

This marked the real beginning of Methodism as a movement—a movement that was to spawn a series of new structures: itinerant preachers, class meetings, societies with per-

* A term used first in the Report of the Section on Unity at the Third Assembly of the World Council of Churches at New Delhi, and in several subsequent ecumenical documents.

sonal and corporate disciplines, circuits, conferences, hymn books. But throughout, the development of new churches was (as here) hesitant, the necessities of mission drawing Wesley and his followers in the path of reluctant ecclesiastical re-formation.

Why this reluctant reform? In eighteenth-century England, the inherited structures of parish life were increasingly failing to meet the necessities of mission, because of their failure to re-form in response to the changing structures of human society. The old village pattern of medieval rural England was beginning to shift toward the world of modern towns and cities. The new communities of coal miners, town dwellers, and shopkeepers were growing up outside the geographical boundaries of rural parish ministration and, worse sociologically and psychologically outside the modes and methods of ministration. Alienated from the old forms and traditions of English life, these harbingers of modern urbanized technological society were outcasts from tradition—alienated also from the care and structures of the church. Their alienated existence cried out for Christian *presence*—cried out for the word of Christ which would come to them with the offer of grace, the grace that offers the promise of true human existence within the reconciled and reconciling family of God in Christ. But the cries went unheeded until at last John Wesley was drawn out on his reluctant path into the byways to offer Christ to the aliens.

Who can say just why the preaching of John Wesley received such a phenomenal response? Perhaps it was because, in their alienation, these lost children of the new age were overwhelmed by the unlikely approach of this proper little aristocrat. In his polished Oxford don's manner, he spoke of God's grace, freely offered to the unworthy; the miracle of the God who came in the form of his only Son and, in the richness of his grace, offered his life to the out casts and the lost. In his very presence Wesley was a sign of that miracle—aristocrat amongst the outcast, scholar amongst the illiterate, polished culture amongst the rowdy, crude mob. He spoke of God's coming down to save, and here was one ready to come down through the rigid class barrier to speak to them of Christ. He told them of Christ, whose love was without limit, going on unbroken to death on the cross; and here was one who came to them with nothing to gain but their hearts, and who stayed with calm assurance through the attacks of mobs and the reproach of the authorities.

They felt lost; he spoke to them of salvation. They felt themselves to be the lowest; he spoke to them of One who comes to the lowest and not only justifies but sanctifies— leading them together into fulness of life in the perfected family of God. They heard him—and believed. In their believing, they forced him to find a way of caring for them. To preach and then to leave them was, he believed, simply "to raise up children for the devil." The newborn in Christ must be nurtured in the family of the faithful; that nurture requires mutual care, with regular attendance on the means of grace by which Christ trains his faithful in the life of fellowship and faith. For that reason, he gathered them into those structures which proved necessary for their growth in grace. The re-formation of structures was the necessary outcome of the response brought forth by the Word.

What determined the path of the reform? How could Wesley decide where he must move beyond the previous structures and provide new ones? This question never ceased to trouble him, and to the end of his days he had to face disturbing questions caused by the tension, nigh unto breaking, resulting from his movement beyond the limits authorized by ecclesiastical authority. But one central vision moved him in the midst of his troubled progress. He was sure that he must be a loyal son of the Church. He was sure that he must stay within the faith once delivered to the saints, sustained by the Holy Spirit in the life of the one Christ, through the means of grace by which Christ continuously feeds the faithful. But he was equally sure that where temporal authorities in the church stood finally in the path of the gospel's mission to the lost, then (having done all he could to move through regular channels) he was required to respond to the call of Christ from the midst of unanswered human need.

In this way Wesley showed himself to be one of those who would insist that we must not only speak of Word and sacraments as marks of the true Church, we must also speak of mission. In Acts 2:42, where the marks of the Church are given, the continuity that is spoken of as essential to the true life of the Church certainly includes Word and sacraments: "they continued in the apostle's teaching and fellowship, and in the breaking of bread and the prayers." But these apostolic Word and sacraments are known *in via*—in the company of the apostles as they go out from that upper room into Jerusalem, and on "to Judaea and to Samaria and to the uttermost parts of the earth." Apostolic Word and sacraments cease to be apostolic when they are removed from that missionary movement. It was this movement—this necessity for the Church to go out to the new shapes of human association and need, in obedience to the missionary call of Christ—that was represented in the re-forming of church life undertaken by Wesley. He was convinced that the Church of England was still sound in Word and sacraments, that her ministry was God-given, and her liturgy "the best that ever there was." But he was equally convinced that, by her imprisonment in the structures of a past age and her refusal to move out to the sheep without a shepherd, she was being untrue to her mission. It was to help overcome this failure, he believed, that God raised him up within the Church and sent him out in irregular paths as an *"extraordinarius"* to arouse the "ordinary" ministers to that godly jealousy by which they would be at last recalled to seek those new forms of obedience their missionary calling demanded.

But by what authority did Wesley seek this re-formation? And by what criteria did he decide upon the forms of missionary obedience that resulted in the Methodist societies? The authority by which he acted was the Word of God as revealed in Christ, given in Scripture and proclaimed in the Church through the centuries. The criteria of judgment were the historic ones, as given in the classical Protestant tradition handed down in the formularies of the Church of England. The criteria by which we are to recognize the true form of the Church are:

1. She must always live by the *instituted means of grace* —that is, the continuing provisions for true Christian life and fellowship instituted by Christ: baptism, the Lord's Supper, prayer (public and private), searching the Scripture, fasting, and "Christian conference."

2. She must also provide the *prudential means of grace* —that is, the changing means by which these unchanging, or instituted, means of grace are brought to the lives of the people in such a way as to enable them to grow up into Christ within the circumstances of their life situation.[2]

The subordination of the *prudential* means to the *instituted* means of grace is necessary for the preservation of true apostolicity. But the translation of the instituted into the prudential is also necessary for the prolongation of true apostolicity. Without that, we fail to heed the apostolic word "Go." Without that, the Word is not brought to men in their changing circumstances in such a way as to take flesh and dwell among them just as surely in the eighteenth century (and the twentieth) as in the first.

It is the interrelation of these instituted and prudential

means of grace that gives the true context for *semper re-formanda*—"the Church always to be reformed," always find-ing that new form with each new day which will enable it to continue to be apostolic. The Church must be *semper reformanda* in order that she may be truly the Body of Christ, in which the people of each new day may grow up into one new man in Jesus Christ as the true presence of Christ comes to them in the midst of the changing structures of their own time.

In the sixteenth century the *semper reformanda* slogan was given its currency. That was no accident. The sixteenth century was the day of dawning for the modern world, in which the relatively static age of medieval Europe began to dissolve into the mobile structures of the cities, with science, industry, and technology gradually coming forth as the chil-dren of the new day. It was only the beginning, but still it was dimly seen that the Church would need to remain in-creasingly open, free to re-form itself in such a way as to be the true presence of Christ with man in his new thought, his new ways of living and associating, his new worlds of decision and action.

In the eighteenth century, again, it is no accident that in Wesley's movement we see a breakthrough in the call to allow the Church to be free to take shape around its mis-sionary calling to the emerging areas of life outside the tradi-tional shapes of the Church. We see this too in the pietism of the eighteenth century which, for all its weaknesses, yearned and learned to free the Church for its new missionary jour-neys into the new worlds that now opened before the pres-sures of trade and commerce. In both cases—Methodism moving to the new classes in the old world, with new forms of church life suited to their condition; and pietism moving to the newly opened territories of the hitherto unknown world—the meaning of *semper reformanda* took on new dimensions. These new dimensions were demanded by the new movements of history; for the eighteenth century marked the surge forward toward the industrial age, and the Church was required to find those ways by which the new shapes of human existence could be approached by the living presence of Christ the Lord. The instituted means of grace required new prudential forms.

Now we are in the twentieth century. As in the sixteenth and eighteenth, we are in the midst of a further powerful surge in historical forces, bringing about a rapid social change which is again forcing us to be aware of the peculiar importance of the *semper reformanda*. With us, the day of industrial technological society has fully come. Now urbanization is a world-wide phenomenon of incredible power. And the revolutions against colonialism, racism, and all forms of caste and segregation signal the widening participation of the rapidly increasing human family in the creativity of nature, and the spreading determination to seek that open society in which none will be excluded from the fruits of his labor. So in our day the changed shapes of human society are calling forth within the Church powerful pressures towards reformation—some perhaps as a true counterforce, to make sure that in the prudential means of grace the true continuities of the instituted means of grace are maintained, but some as demonic forces resisting the Spirit as it seeks to give us freedom for our mission.

It is, however, in the very nature of the gospel that we should be free in the sense of being open to the future. The New Testament speaks of the coming of Christ into the world as introducing a restless ferment of ceaseless change. "The old has passed away, the new has come" (2 Cor. 5:17). The nature of this new life "in Christ" is radically different from the ordinary life men lead. Natural human communities erect barriers of prestige, or class, or culture, or race, or language. But "in Christ there is no Greek or Jew, no bond or free, no male or female, no barbarian or Scythian." Natural human communities are dominated by self-interest, but "in Christ each esteems the other better than himself." As a result, the presence of this new life of the new age means the introduction of a ferment of constant change into the human communities of the world (Col. 3:1-15; 1 John 3:2), and even into our relationship to the world of nature (Rom. 8:19-25).

The Church, then, is to be the sign of this new fermenting presence of Christ in the midst of the communities of the world. In her life the world is meant to see an "earnest," or "first fruits," of the final transformation. Because of this calling to be the sign, or first fruits, of the coming kingdom, the very nature of the Christian community is to be open to the future, with its life as an embodiment of its hope. The place of the Church, therefore, is out in the midst of the changes of life, joyfully witnessing to the Christ who makes all things new; to the Christ who opens the way to the future by overcoming the principalities and powers which enslave us to the old, to the past. Of course the changes that are occurring in the world are not by any means all changes which are bringing us nearer to the kingdom of God. But they are changes in which Christ the Lord of history is at work, and in which he is working out his purpose. The task of the Church is to be with him in this work, pointing the world to its true Lord and joining with Christ in his battle against the demonic forces that would seek to turn the promise of change into new forms of enslavement. The task of the Church is to be in the midst of change, seeking by word, deed, and presence to witness to Christ the Lord, who alone is the future and who alone can make all things new.

The Church, however, as a community in the midst of the communities of the world also is tempted to become a prisoner to the past, a community that loses its missionary calling by ceasing to be open to the future. For this reason, judgment must begin in the house of God. Christ must first perform his freeing work in the Church, in order that she may be the true witness to the world. *Semper reformanda* is thus a description of the calling of the Church. If she is to be always the same—in the sense of being a witness to the Christ who is the same yesterday, today, and forever—she must always be being changed. She must be an emerging sign of the new day, a sign of a community in which the love of God is casting out those worldly fears which resist the dawning of the new age.

In the eighteenth century, the Church of England was largely a prisoner to its past. In the world, the work of God in bringing about those ceaseless changes in which man was being offered new hope (or new despair) was leaving the church behind. Its missionary task of being in the midst of those changes witnessing to the Lord of history was largely unfulfilled. Judgment had to begin in the house of God. In the work of John Wesley this judgment came, calling the church out of its slavery to past form, into the free life of the people of God whose place is in the midst of the emerging world, showing forth "the works of him who has called you out of darkness into his marvelous light." In Methodism the given means of grace were able to take form within the life of the commercial towns and industrial villages that signaled the beginning of that vast movement which is now the twentieth century.

Methodism, however, was only the sign of God's call to the Church to find new form—certainly it was not in itself the fulfillment! Wesley was right when he saw himself and his societies as "extraordinary," as "raised up to arouse the ordinary messengers to jealousy." He did not see Methodism as itself the Church, but as societies raised up by God to recall the Church to her missionary task. For that reason it was a sad day for the Church of England when Methodism was forced out and became a society in search of the Church. For that meant that the Church of England had largely missed the day of visitation, and it meant also that Methodism had an unfulfilled destiny which she has ever since been in perilous danger of forgetting, the destiny of witnessing to the need for the Church to be free for the future: *semper reformanda*.

The Church is to be the pilgrim people, moving on to the city which is to come; on the way we are to pitch temporary tents, in which our life together will be a sign of the coming kingdom. But constantly we must be on the watch to hear the call of the Master of the caravan as he summons us to move out with him on that restless march to the end. What an irony, then, that Methodism, which was raised up as a sign of this movement of the Church into the future, should become in so many places today a symbol of imprisonment to the past. The Church today, in the midst of twentieth-century change, is called to be the sign of that new life in which the middle walls of hostility shall be overcome between white and black, cultured and uncultured, rich and poor. But Methodism in the U.S.A., with its rigid separation of Negro from white and its jurisdictional system for the protection of sectional interests, has become the symbol of imprisonment to the dying culture. Instead of being the first fruits of the new humanity, it is in danger of becoming the final guardian of the rotting fruit of the old age of segregation and sectionalism.

Of course there are in Methodism many signs of hope, in the U.S.A. as well as in other countries. In South Africa, for example, the Methodist Church has taken its stand against apartheid and, by appointing an African as president of the Conference, has given symbolic witness to the call of the church to witness in its life to the purpose of Christ to enable mankind to grow up together as "one new man." In the United States too, there are centers of renewal within the church. But by and large it must be confessed that Methodism is failing to be true to her calling.

John Wesley, as Gordon Rupp has reminded us, was an apostle of grace. His constant theme was that we must set no limits to the extent to which Christ can move us on towards sanctification. His "optimism of grace" expressed a faith in the power of Christ to enable our lives to surge into the future, moving on to the goal of our high calling in Christ. And this sanctification is not simply in personal virtues; it is displayed in the life of the community. It was characteristic of Methodists, therefore, to be always on the move. "The King's business required haste." Their preachers were itinerants; they had to keep up with what God was doing in the world. In their methods they were constantly experimenting, not by contrived dissemination of gimmicks, but by the imaginative discovery of new ways to meet the new needs of the changing world. Sunday schools for the illiterate; training for employment; credit to offer a new start in the world; clinics to bring hope to those society ignored—all these witness to the restless readiness of these Methodists to seek to show forth in the life of their fellowship the power of Christ to offer true hope in the midst of the world's despair and false hopes. And to fulfill that missionary task, they knew that they must be ready to be the "presence of Christ" within the changing shapes of human need.

Now in the twentieth century, as we have seen, there are massive changes in the shapes of human need, and the *semper reformanda* means that again we face the need for major restructuring of the shape of the Church's life in order that it may be the first fruits of the new creation. There is every sign that we are in a period in which the changes are every whit as great as those of the sixteenth and eighteenth centuries. But of course there are big differences in both the type of response that is needed and the nature of the response that is emerging in the Church.

The Required Response

The nature of the response that is required is the subject of a major study authorized by the World Council of Churches Third Assembly at New Delhi. The Study is entitled "The Missionary Structure of the Congregation," * and its task is to explore the forms of church life needed for the fulfillment of the contemporary missionary task. In the course of the study, a consensus seems to be emerging that the Church is at present too much turned in upon itself,† so much concerned with the maintenance of its own life that it is not free to be with God in his work in and for the world. So it is stressed that we must seek those new forms of church life that will enable us to be the presence of Christ at the places where the world brings men together—at the places where decisions are made, where anxieties are formed, and where the fabric of society is being woven.‡ What makes the required response so radical is that urbanization has brought into being a mobile world, in which such public worlds as politics, busi-

---

* The Study is carried on by the Department on Studies in Evangelism, through working groups in several different parts of the world. From these studies, a report is being prepared for presentation to the Central Committee of the WCC and finally to the Fourth Assembly. To enable local groups to participate fully in this important study, I have prepared two study books: *Where in the World?* and *What in the World?*. Both are available from the Central Department of Evangelism, NCC, 475 Riverside Drive, New York, New York 10027.

† One of the classical descriptions of sin is *cor incurvatum in se* ("the heart turned in upon itself"), in contrast to the true life in which man is freed from self-concern and freed for the neighbor. So too the church that is curved in upon itself is a church that is not free for God's mission for others in the world.

‡ In Chapter IV of *What in the World?*, an attempt is made to point to promising signs of the new forms of presence which God is bringing forth. These are called "Parables of Missionary Presence," in order to emphasize the fact that these examples are not blueprints to be copied, but are examples by which Christ seeks to train our eyes and ears to see and hear the calls which he brings to us from the midst of the needs of the world.

ness, commerce, mass communications, and leisure have been separated from the world of residence. The Church, however, has inherited a congregational form that centers on residence. It finds itself alienated to a large extent from the mobile public worlds, unable to give adequate witness by word, deed, and presence to the lordship of Christ in the midst of the events of contemporary history. The alienation, of course, is not complete; but there is an increasing awareness of the extent of the separation, and an agonizing awareness of the extent also of the imprisonment of our energies in maintaining the internal structure of our introverted churches. What is needed, then, is a turning of the life of the churches inside out, a conversion by which we are restored to an awareness that our missionary calling is to "go" and to be the servant presence of Christ in the world.

The Response That Is Emerging

If the nature of the Church's response to the events of the twentieth century is different from the responses required in the sixteenth and eighteenth centuries, so also the response that is emerging reflects that difference. Here we need mention only a few of the major features of present response.

1. The Ecumenical Movement is in one aspect a response to the growing awareness of the emergence of a world community in which different races, cultures, and classes are being thrown together to an extent never before dreamed.

In the relatively static world of the pre-industrial age, the divisions of the Church were not so serious. The Church in each place still had power to witness to Christ's lordship over the whole of life. But now the mobility of the world, with the vast changes in social structures and the development of new worlds of thought and action—such as modern education, technology, and industry, each with its own secular unity—has seriously damaged the witnessing power of our divided churches. In this situation we are becoming sensitive to the missionary calling of the Church to proclaim to the world Christ's power to reveal the unity of life's meaning and to overcome the hostilities of worldly communities, leading men into the fulfillment of life in the one family of God. Here Christ is calling us out of the isolations of our past into the unity of our missionary calling in the world.

2. There has been a remarkable growth of concern with the ministry of the laity—a concern that is truly ecumenical.* It has become clear that if the Church is to be the presence of Christ, witnessing to him by word and deed at the places where decisions are made, anxieties formed, and energies extended, this task must be fulfilled by the laity within the secular world. The New Testament speaks of the whole *laos* as ministers, with each receiving the grace needed for the fulfillment of his ministry, and with the Church being responsible for stirring up these gifts in order to equip the saints for their missionary obedience. Now we are witnessing a widespread search for ways in which these ministries may be understood, trained, and fulfilled.

3. There is a burgeoning appearance of new forms of missionary presence in the world. For a few years it seemed as though the quoting of examples led only to repetition—Iona, worker priests, East Harlem, were constantly on the lips of the prophets of renewal. But now their name is legion,† and in many parts of the world the Church is seeking to break out of its isolation and find creative ways of ap-

---

* The books on it come equally from Roman Catholic and Protestant, from established and Free Church, from old world and new; and it is difficult to tell from the writing which is which! The bulletins of the Department of the Laity of the WCC are an invaluable source of information concerning this development.

† See *What in the World?*, Chapter IV, for an attempt to analyze the types of "experiment" such as "Response to Crisis Need," "Approaches to Man at the Points of His Strength," "Responsible Planning"; also an attempt to ask whether there are certain characteristics which are essential to genuine forms of missionary presence.

proaching the different aspects of modern life in their own
integrity and of revealing to the world the presence of its
Lord as he goes about his work of leading history on to its
conclusion.

In these responses we may see the signs of response
in the Church and know that there is some awareness of the
true mission of the Church. But in these responses we must
see the signs of judgment as well as promise; for we know
that all too often the Church is resisting the Spirit, that again
it seems unaware of the days of its visitation. Thus the Ecumenical Movement spreads, and we are aware that here the
pressure of the Spirit is being felt. And yet the Ecumenical
Movement is kept at arm's length, with our churches continuing to protect their separate lives even when they confess
with their lips that we are called to do everything together
except where we are still compelled by conscientious conviction to act separately. And again, the emphasis on the ministry
of the laity grows, but too often this is subjected to pitiful
perversion, by encouraging laymen to feel that they are fulfilling their ministry if they give more time inside the church
institution instead of being trained there for their ministries
in the world. Then, too, new forms of missionary presence
appear that are parables through which Christ seeks to open
our eyes and ears so that we may respond with imaginative
forms of servant presence in the communities of our calling.
But all too often we speak of these as "experiments" and calm
our consciences, in the face of our failure in obedience, by
pointing to them as proof that the Church is not failing to
meet the new calls of the day.

The Methodist Response

In response to the need for unity, Methodism, like most
churches, has a mixed record. In "mission" work it has
moved well, but mostly in British areas. In Western areas,

again in common with most other churches, her record is not impressive. In Canada, yes—union with Presbyterians and Congregationalists. In Britain, negotiations with the Church of England, with a proposed scheme for gradual unity. But there the signs are ominous, with the arguments against union revealing far more slavery to the past than freedom for the future. In the U.S.A., the unity in Methodism gained in 1939 created a vast organization. But it must be confessed that external unity simply covered up inner conflicts concerning the nature and mission of the church, and that until these inner demons are exorcized there is little hope of Methodism taking a creative role in the movement towards that unity which will enable the Church to fulfill its missionary task of revealing to the world the true unity in Christ which can bring reconciliation across the dividing walls of present hostility. In American Methodism the jurisdictional system is simply a confession that "unity" could be gained in 1939 only at the price of unresolved sectional and racial suspicion and conflict. In this way Methodism confessed that in her life she was not able to show the world that it is Christ's purpose that these conflicts should be broken down. Until she resolutely faces these inward contradictions, which so often tie the hands of the Church and prevent her from taking her place in witnessing to the new life which Christ is seeking to bring forth in the midst of the old world, Methodism will be able to make little contribution to continuing ecumenical growth in the U.S.A.

In the call to discern the ministries of the laity in the secular world, and train them accordingly, again Methodism has nothing impressive to record—and this in a church that arose with the assertion of the freedom of the laity to exercise ministries of responsibility for the church. There would seem to be historical reasons for this. As the societies of Methodism gradually separated from the Anglican Church, the lay preachers gradually assumed full clerical status; and in the search for ecclesiastical identity the tightly knit system of Methodism exposed her to the peculiar danger of developing institutional programs under clerical control. The effectiveness of these programs was judged by the extent to which laymen could be brought to participate in in-group activities. For that reason the need to develop lay ministries in the world could easily be overlooked. Of course there have been many attempts to move out. The creative activity of Methodists in both England and the U.S.A. in the social gospel movement of the late nineteenth and early twentieth centuries was a breakthrough of the spirit of earlier Methodist vision. But in recent years the spirit of self-conscious institutionalism seems to have gained ascendancy over the original vocation to be a sign of the freedom of the *laos* to move out with Christ into the changing shapes of life.

Similarly, Methodism manifests at this point, to a tragic degree, a lack of freedom. We can point to a few creative figures such as Alan Walker in Sydney, with his acute sense of the need for changing forms of ministry in the modern metropolis. But in general it must be confessed that Methodism is living more from its evangelical past than towards the new missionary imperatives. There is the danger, of course, in ecumenical discussion, for a writer to be tempted to engage in denominational self-flagellation in order to appear humble. If others can see more signs of hope in the contemporary Methodist scene, I will rejoice.

That there are strong evidences of judgment beginning in the house of God, and of Methodists in many places fighting for the true freedom for the Word of God to move us out to our new places of obedience, must be acknowledged with joy. That God has not abandoned us, I am sure. That he is working within us, to awaken us to the final witness which he seeks from us before he allows us to disappear into the larger life of his church family, I am equally certain. But it would be folly to cover up the extent of the resistance to these forces of renewal in the form of institutional inertia and, worse, in the determined grasping of the forms of the past.

As an Australian, perhaps I can be permitted to witness to a proposal which I believe symbolizes the true missionary calling of Methodists in the world of today. It is the proposal for church union in Australia, put forward jointly by Methodists, Presbyterians, and Congregationalists, and due to be voted on in the next three years. Again it must be confessed that there is no guarantee of acceptance. But whether accepted or not in this first try, it still represents an attempt to face the call of Christ to move out in the ways we have discussed, and to allow that missionary calling to be expressed in the very form of the church's life.*

As the Commission on Church Union asked itself what form of church life was needed for the fulfillment of our missionary calling today, it was recognized that the church in Australia had to be seen in its setting in the Asian world. The policy which has kept Australia white represents a missionary calling for the church. How can the church be the first fruits of the kingdom and reveal the purpose of Christ to break through these barriers of human pride, fear, and suspicion? The answer to that question was seen to lie in seeking a form of church life which will reveal the unity of the church across racial lines. The result of that quest is a proposed

---

* The negotiations in Australia were not able to include the Church of England. That church achieved a national constitution only toward the end of the negotiations, and is not yet able to participate officially. Consultants from the Church of England, however, were present at many sessions, and the proposal was designed with the hope that it would open the way to union with them in the near future. This is explained in the Report of the Joint Commission on Church Union, "The Church—Its Nature, Function and Ordering, together with Proposed Basis of Union," published in 1963, by The Aldersgate Press, 430 Little Collins Street, Melbourne, C.1.

Concordat of Unity with the Church of South India, which will bring into the form of the church's life unity-in-mission across the barriers of race, language, culture, class, and custom. Ministers would be interchangeable, resources shared, and witness would be given in the church's life that the unity of the life of Christ must not be limited by the arbitrary and sinful limitations to human community that have been imposed by the world.

But why the Church of South India? And why a form of unity which creates an episcopate and unites it with that of the C.S.I.? Because the form of unity already achieved in the C.S.I. is seen as having prophetic significance. Here, the Commission judged, God has set before us a sign on the path into the freedom of the future, which provides true continuities with the fulness of the Church's past life, and opens the way to true freedom for our unity-in-mission in the contemporary world. To quote the report:

The two preoccupations of the Commission are brought together in the proposal which we now put forward; namely, a preoccupation with the call of God upon us to fulfill the mission of this hour; and, a preoccupation with the fulness of the Church's faith and order. The two are not finally separable: they are one. The Church is given the fulness of the apostolic faith and the equipment of ordered ministry in order that she may fulfill her mission. . . .

There are important theological reasons why we should see the C.S.I. as a prophetic sign established by God in our midst:

(i) In the C.S.I. the three traditions which our negotiating churches represent have already accepted episcopacy. They did so, it is true, at the point of union with a part of the Anglican Church; but for many the reason for this acceptance was not a concession to Anglican sentiment, but a conviction that this is a part of God's good will for the life of his Church. Subsequent

experience has convinced even the hesitant; and it would be possible to quote many ex-Congregationalists, ex-Methodists, and
ex-Presbyterians, to show how experience of episcopacy as prac-
tised in South India has confirmed them in this conviction. It is
a fact with which we must come to terms that in the C.S.I. the
gulf between episcopal and non-episcopal churches has been
bridged. The question is: what do we make of that sign? An
isolated instance in church history, or a finger pointing forward
prophetically?

(ii) In the C.S.I. episcopacy was accepted as an important
strand in the coming unity which is God's will for his Church,
but in such a way as to accept unambiguously the ministries of
the churches to which we belong as genuine ministries of Christ
blest and ordered by him. This was done, along with a common
agreement that the way forward together was in a unity which
took up those ministries and what was called "the historic episcopate," so that the whole would in future bear God's Word and
sacraments and care to men.

(iii) In the C.S.I. episcopacy was reformed in the direction
of 'bishop-in-presbytery.' This delivered both the Church of England and the other uniting churches from a narrowly juridical
view of the Church by a recovery of the sense of the Body and
the service and function of its various parts. We gratefully ob-
serve the way in which a church in an environment other than
Western Europe has shed some of the less admirable characteristics of 'Western' thinking and has sought to give expression to
a more profoundly biblical and patristic understanding of the
function of the bishop-in-presbytery.

For these reasons we believe that the C.S.I. has been raised
up by God to open a way in the movement toward church unity.
We believe also that by offering to enter with her into this Concordat, as an expression of the unity of the Church in mission,
across racial, national, and cultural lines, we shall be helping to
deepen the symbolic significance of the C.S.I. This is not simply

a matter of being called by God to move out to the C.S.I. as givers. We are in need; and the Australian churches by themselves, or even together, are unlikely to receive the renewal and reorientation required of us in this present hour. And we believe therefore that this Concordat with the C.S.I. could open up the way to a new movement forward, which could spread to other churches in our region and which could weld together unity and mission to an extent not previously possible.

The Commission recognises that decisions such as this, which involve reading the 'signs' of what God is doing in his Church and in his world, are decisions fraught with peril. There is no escape, however, from such decisions. The necessity to interpret the signs is placed upon us by Our Lord, and all the Commission asks is that the members of the churches should share in this task, praying that in accordance with his promise, God will grant the guidance that is needed in testing the spirits to see whether they are from him. The judgment that God is calling the three negotiating Churches into unity with each other and into a Concordat with the C.S.I. is now offered to the churches, asking only that the members allow themselves the opportunity to explore this proposal carefully so that they may make a responsible judgment under the guidance of the Spirit.

In the attempt to allow the form of the church's life to express that calling to mission-in-unity which will best provide for missionary presence in the world setting in which she finds herself, the Australian Commission was driven also to attempts to open the way to the true ministries of the laity in the secular world of today. One way in which it attempts to provide for this is by a permanent order of deacons, through which the ministries of Word and sacrament can be related more effectively to these ministries in the world.

'Deacons' have normally been those designated for the exercise of the Church's ministry of service to the world—the care of the

poor, the sick, and others in need—although sometimes the office
has been narrowed by becoming predominantly concerned with
the property and finance of the congregation.

We believe that the important insight represented by the
Reformed office of ordained elders is that it takes into the oversight of the congregation representative laity who are involved
in the vocations of the world, and symbolises also the reaching
out of the ministry of the church into the secular occupations of
everyday life. The time of union provides an opportunity for
a creative re-interpretation and broadening of this valuable form
of the ministry, so that members of the laity can be admitted to
the diaconate, participating with the presbyters in the oversight
of the congregation, and also reaching out into the ordinary vocations of life there to exercise their ministry of oversight and
leadership among their fellow Christians in the world.

Similarly the report seeks to provide for the freedom in
church order that is needed to move out into the new sociological realms of our urban society.

In asking the question as to the form and order that the
church should assume if it is to fulfill the mission of Christ, we
must take seriously the particular setting in which the Australian
Church finds itself. For example:

We must examine the sociological changes that have occurred in Australian life, such as the rapid urbanisation, the development of suburbia, the separation of man's place of living
from his place of working, and the rise of highly institutionalised
forms of specialised life—in education, health, commerce, industry, mass media, etc. We must then ask whether these require
different forms of congregational life, new types of ministry,
changed structures of church government.

The report notes further:

In recognising the necessity for the basic ministry of the Word and sacraments within the congregation, we must also be open to the possibility that new forms of congregational life will arise which will call for new ways of carrying out this ministry. There has developed in our society an increasing separation between man's place of abode and the places where men pursue their economic, political, and social life, and seek the fulfillment of their needs for education, health, and recreation. Our present congregational life is almost exclusively related to the former. We must be ready to experiment with forms of congregational life which will provide for the presence of the Christian fellowship at those crucial places where decisions are made, energies expended, and attachments formed.

To make further provision for the freedom needed to fulfill the mission of the church in the new sociological worlds of contemporary life, the report calls for built-in flexibility in the modes of government.

The possibility should be kept open that the regions for which bishops are given responsibility could include, as well as the traditional geographical region, sociological regions such as industry, education, health institutions, or oversight of areas of work now carried on by departments of the church. It might be proper also, for the church to adopt such new forms of oversight as team episcopacy, in which several bishops, each with responsibility for a group of presbyters working in contiguous areas of different geographical and sociological types, may co-ordinate their work and planning in order that the power of Christ may enable diverse groups to grow into unity in him across their human divisions. The Constitution should leave the way open for considerable flexibility in this matter.

Here, I believe, is a creative response in one small section of Methodism to the missionary imperatives placed before it. It points the way, I further believe, to the kind of response to which we all are called, "each in his own place."

6

Lewis S. Mudge:

Can Presbyterians Be Reformed?

The current effort to bring about reform within the Roman Catholic Church is an exciting sign for all Christians that the Holy Spirit is at work among us. No one knows, of course, how fast or how far this reformation of the Roman Church will go. But the fact that such a movement exists at all is impressive. Karl Barth raises an inevitable question when he asks whether the churches of the Protestant Reformation are anywhere near as serious about reform as Rome now appears to be. And Father Küng is surely justified in asking Protestants to respond with something more than suspicious, yet fascinated, amazement. Protestants must once more begin thinking seriously about what continuing reformation according to the Word of God means to them.

The New Reformation and Ecumenical Strategy

It would be misleading, of course, to suggest that while Rome has been stirring, Protestantism has been asleep. Long before the Council was convened, Protestant writers were speaking of the Ecumenical Movement as offering the possibility of a "new reformation." Acting more or less together, the Protestant and Eastern Orthodox churches have achieved insights which have revolutionary potential. Significant changes have been brought about in the life and outlook of Protestantism in particular, and more are clearly on the way. But at the same time, this ecumenical reformation has not penetrated far enough into the life of the churches as such. The more closely one looks at the actual participation of most Protestant denominations in ecumenical affairs, the clearer it becomes that the ecumenical dimension of church life is regarded as an interesting option or specialty toward which *some* people are drawn: one interest among others vying for attention in already overcrowded ecclesiastical agendas. While the boards and agencies of the churches have often been responsive to ecumenical thinking in the realms of program- and curriculum-planning, it could hardly be said that many Protestant bodies have been led to reconsider their ecclesiological assumptions and constitutional structures. The new reformation which Father Küng and many others are seeking surely has to do with this latter, virtually untouched, level of action.

Ecumenically minded Protestants have been reluctant to press for major changes in the constitutions of their own churches, at least partly because they have felt that these structures are bound soon to be superseded. They have felt that the great opportunity for reform will come in the process of working out the constitution of a united Church. But union negotiations have been going on for some years now without overwhelming success. And those union plans which have come to fruition have not brought with them many very radical changes in the structure and outlook of the bodies concerned. The picture has been largely one of mutual adjustment and accommodation: painful enough for some, but hardly world-shaking in the light of the challenges to Christianity posed by a world "come of age." Possibly the Holy Spirit, wiser than we, is making us wait until our unions can be much more inclusive. Perhaps it is God's purpose that success should elude us until we are ready to discuss a common life with Roman Catholic and Orthodox Christians as well as with our fellow Protestants. But perhaps, on the other hand, what is holding us up is the fact that *we* are not yet fit, in God's sight, to be united with *anyone* in Christ! Perhaps we will not be allowed to succeed in our union efforts until we become churches whose union will not simply amalgamate our various forms of faithlessness on an unprecedented scale.

We have good reason to wonder, therefore, whether we may not have put too much confidence in the effort to achieve Protestant unity, and not enough in the effort to rediscover the meaning of the gospel "in each place." It is beginning to be felt among the younger generation of Protestant church leadership, for example, that the Faith and Order enterprise, despite its new interest in the "local," actually has a vested interest in keeping alive questions which are no longer real for most Christians. Practitioners of Faith and Order, it is said, are pursuing a kind of dialogue which is increasingly remote from the growing edge of the Church. The very discussion of denominational divisions seems somehow to presuppose that the existing denominational forms have some kind of relative validity, when the truth is that we have a revolution on our hands which may well sweep away all our existing structures. Such allegations against the Faith and Order movement are, of course, not really fair. Faith and Order is a great deal more awake to the contemporary situation than some younger churchmen appear to think. Yet the whole union movement is forced to deal with that situation in strangely oblique terms. Division among the Protestant denominations is an anachronism that ought to have been eliminated a decade ago, but remains to plague us in an age when the problems facing the Church are much more vast.

As things stand now, the power to make decisions which will truly transform the posture of Protestantism in the modern world still rests with the separate denominations. That, I suppose, is why it is valid for me to approach the question of a new reformation from the standpoint of my own church. But let it be said at once that I do not regard anything I will say here as an argument for continuing the separate existence of Presbyterianism one moment longer than is absolutely necessary. Significant internal debates will inevitably divert denominations from the larger union effort, and there may in some cases be good reason to delay serious union conversations until these internal questions are resolved. I would say, for example, that the elimination of all forms of racial discrimination from the structure of a church could well be made a precondition for participation in *any* responsible interchurch activities. But it is specious to argue that the cause either of reunion or renewal is advanced by unilateral efforts to make ourselves "better Methodists" or "better Presbyterians" in isolation from each other.

Anything said here about reform within Presbyterianism, then, is said with our brothers of other branches of the one Church in mind. There must be a catholic dimension in all that we say and do, such that we recognize our responsibility to act in behalf of the whole Body of Christ in the particular places where we minister. If, for example, one considers the Presbyterian ordering of Holy Communion, it is indispensable to remember that this liturgy, comparatively simple though it may be, *represents* a body of insight and tradition shared by the whole Church which is incomparably richer and fuller than what that particular form of words can actually express. If, therefore, I write about reformation from a Presbyterian standpoint, it is with a sense of being in constant dialogue with my brothers throughout the Church catholic. In what follows it will be evident how much I have learned from them.

Reformation and the "Reformed Tradition"

The reformation we are talking about is no mere modernization. It is no mere adjustment of well-worn ways to meet new conditions. What is needed is some response to the realization that we are not communicating the gospel any more by what we say or by what we are. This point has been made by a multitude of writers, and the general outlines of the position are reasonably clear. The world has grown up to the extent that it can now speak for itself without any theologian telling it what it "really means." Secular fields of knowledge and endeavor have earned their autonomy over against the ecclesiastical establishment. Meanwhile, society has reorganized itself in forms with which our parish and denominational structures were never meant to cope. The "new creation" which God has brought into being is the metropolis, while our congregations continue to function most successfully within the P.T.A. syndrome. In their more violent forms, these changes in our world add up to revolution, while in the Church it is too often "business as usual." These are serviceable generalizations, even if they do not apply equally well to all situations. We can count on the problem becoming more, rather than less, acute, and it is time for something radical to be done about it.

Such questions have been faced in my church mainly in the seminaries, in some of the boards and agencies (notably those concerned with Christian education, mission, and ecumenical relations), and in various experimental projects, usually done jointly with other denominations. So far as I can see, there has been less attention to these issues in the judicatories: the sessions of local churches, presbyteries, synods, and the General Assembly. At least one attempt has been made, however, with General Assembly authorization and support, to focus these problems for every Presbyterian. A study, with complex ramifications, of the question of Church and state was sent to the presbyteries during 1962-63, with the request that there be organized study of the document during one or more Presbytery meetings and that expressions of opinion on a number of specific questions be transmitted to the Assembly. The response to this effort has been positive enough to suggest that the Church may well try the same method on some other question. Furthermore, one cannot underestimate the effect on the whole United Presbyterian Church of the leadership in civil rights matters recently shown by the top officials of the denomination. This has served to dramatize the issues facing the church as little else could.

It has become clear, however, that Presbyterians are divided on these matters. It is still not clear to many that we *do* live in a revolutionary time, and attempts to respond to the world situation in the name of the gospel are often viewed as a kind of apostasy, or at best as evidence of a strange predilection for the *avant garde*. The nature of this division in the church came out very clearly at the 18th General Council of the World Presbyterian Alliance in 1959 at São Paulo, Brazil, where communication between the two schools of thought became all but impossible. There is reason to expect that the phenomenon may be even more pronounced during the summer of 1964, when the Alliance meets again at Frankfurt-am-Main. I am inclined to think that *this*, rather than any other form of the ecumenical question, will prove to be the vital issue for Presbyterians over the next decade. No doubt it will be the issue for other denominations as well. And there is no reason to suppose that this issue is not as potentially divisive as any faced by the Church in the course of its long history.

It is probably impossible for a writer who personally stands so far on the side of "revolution" to be fair. I do not believe, however, that this is a matter which can or should be settled by parliamentary compromise. Fortunately, the theological structure of this debate is still very fluid. Those on the side of the revolution, and therefore of radical reformation, have certainly not worked out the theological implications of their intuitions. If the church can maintain, and perhaps enhance, its openness to experimentation, meanwhile exploring its own tradition for resources to meet the contemporary situation, there *need* be no schism or disintegration of the body.

It is by no means self-evident, of course, that churches of the "Reformed" heritage have any special advantage where it comes to thinking out what reformation means today. It is probable that the theological insights which were vehicles for the sixteenth-century Reformation will turn out to be only indirectly applicable to the questions we face now. Reformation theology probably contributed most to the possibility of continuing Christian renewal by the encouragement it gave men to believe in their calling to upset established orders where these seemed contrary to the Word of God. Historians have suggested, not without drawing criticism, that the doctrines of election and of salvation by grace alone are inherently antifeudal and antihierarchical in that they encourage men from the bottom of the heap to see themselves as worthy in the sight of God as those on top. This is the stuff of which revolutions have been made, from Moses to Cromwell and onward.

But there is more to it than that. Reformation theology

substituted dynamic for static categories as vehicles with which to understand the presence of God in the world. The great theological achievement of the patristic period and of its medieval aftermath was that it worked out what it means to affirm the real presence of God in a world seen as a static constellation of substances, essences, and *personae.* The achievement of the Reformation was to succeed in proclaiming the real presence of God in human existence, seen as a realm of freedom and grace. The freedom involved here, of course, was and is *God's* freedom. The point was not that man was liberated to exercise his sole private judgment in matters of ecclesiology, economics, or exegesis, but that the freedom of *God* to call men to new forms of service in the Church and in the world took on tangible meaning.

It is significant that the effects of this new awareness were, from the beginning, more revolutionary in social and political matters than they were in church affairs. It is a commonplace that the Reformation faith has had something to do with social change in an impressive variety of situations, from the rise of the European bourgeoisie to the anticolonialist revolutions of our own day in Africa, Asia, and Latin America—not to speak of the civil rights revolution in the United States. But it is notorious that the Protestant churches have been slow to react internally to these signs of the power of the gospel. In fact, Protestantism has had little idea what to do from any point of view about the social revolutions it has helped to touch off. Luther's frantic tirade against the "thieving murderous horde of peasants" has been repeated often enough in effect since.

There has been something wrong with Protestant understandings of the relation between Church and world. On the one hand, Protestantism has encouraged the world to find its own voice, its own autonomy, over against the Church as an institution. This has *not* meant that the world has been abandoned to become godless, but rather that the world, quite apart from the Church, has been understood as a theater of the glory of God. But then the Church has continued to understand itself in a fundamentally medieval way, *as if* the ecclesiastical institution still somehow retained its monopoly upon affairs of the Spirit. In the West, society has until very recently been willing to allow ecclesiastical establishments to retain at least the outward accouterments of the old hegemony, so that the ordinary man could be pardoned if he came to share the illusion of the ecclesiastics that God lived in church and nowhere else. But not being particularly interested in *that* kind of God, the ordinary man has transformed his freedom in God's secular world into the claim to be free of God altogether. Thus Protestantism has largely failed to communicate the salient point of Reformation theology: that God *is* in the world, that he always has been and always will be, and that he, in his sovereign freedom, offers his grace and favor directly to men even apart from the merit of "church membership."

What kind of ecclesiology really does go with the thought of the Reformation? One proposal has been to make the doctrine of justification by faith apply to the Church as well as to the individual.[1] The effect of this would seem to be to range religious institutions along with other social structures under the judgment and grace of God. The proposal is attractive, but I am not sure that it is as helpful as it seems for the specific purpose at hand. It is one thing to argue, as Professor T. F. Torrance and Bishop Lesslie Newbigin have done, that the Church *is* the Church only by God's grace. That is perfectly true, and it is a valuable principle to keep in mind in ecumenical conversations. But *what* the Church is by the grace of God is different from what other social structures are by God's grace. The words "secular" and "secularized" may apply to the Church as well as to the world, but if they do, they apply in a modified sense. And that is what we are still seeking to grasp.

It is perhaps comforting to be able to define the needed twentieth-century reformation of the Church as something toward which the sixteenth-century Reformation at least points. But whether anything more can be squeezed out of the old theological categories is another matter. Part of the problem is that although these words speak to us as theologians, they are already ceasing to speak to us as twentieth-century men, and they never have spoken very adequately to most men alive today.

One of the reasons for this, and incidentally for the continued medievalism of our ecclesiology, may well be the connection of both with habits of thought which regard the Christian faith as something essentially "supernatural." If we have discarded the social hierarchy of medieval life, we have nevertheless retained a sense of metaphysical hierarchy in our theological imagery. We must face the fact that the erosion of the position of the Church in modern society has something to do with modern man's rejection of the "supernatural" as a separate realm of being in which the Church can somehow be at home. And *we* are modern men. Again, we cannot reduce the Church to being one social institution among many, any more than the incarnate Christ can be merely one man among many. But it takes very little change in the previous sentence to make it read "one man *for* many," and here we are on the track of the truth.

One further point, and a very important one. We probably have no idea just how bourgeois our theological habits must seem to be from the standpoint of people who live outside our comfortable suburban enclaves. I am told that for the Negro American, the doctrine of justification is so easily identified as the source of the white man's complacency and readiness to oppress and exploit darker-skinned peoples that it is no longer serviceable as a means of communicating the gospel. Furthermore, our complex ecclesiastical structures are so grounded in the social status quo as to be well-nigh impervious to modification by revised understandings of the received tradition in any form. It is assumed in our Church that we know what the Protestant tradition means. But the great Reformation words have become flattened and de-natured. Their capacity to bring about change is spent. The door to change is, of course, open. But the impetus will have to come from new thinking, new imagery, new inspiration by the Holy Spirit which takes into account the life, not just of Protestants of European ancestry, but of all the people of God.

Reformation and Theological Imagination

The imaginative thinking we need is beginning to appear. One of the most intriguing suggestions describes the needed transformation in our thought as a shift from a Temple-on-Mount-Zion psychology to a "diaspora" outlook in which the people of God are scattered throughout a pagan and hostile culture. Richard Shaull, in his inaugural address as Professor of Ecumenics at Princeton Theological Seminary,[2] has been possibly the first to make a truly thoroughgoing use of this concept. Likening the thousand years of "Christen-dom" to the life of Israel gathered about the Temple in Jerusalem, Professor Shaull compares the era on which we are entering to the scattering of the Exile and the subsequent growth of an entirely new kind of form for the life of Israel, the diaspora type synagogue. Professor Shaull is not merely suggesting that Christians are gathered on Sunday and scat-tered during the week, but *that the Church as such is in a diaspora situation.* There is no place where it is "at home."

So pregnant is this diaspora image that I would like to

suggest some further ramifications which the biblical materials seem to suggest. One thinks at once not only of Babylon, where the children of Israel were forced to sing the songs of Zion "in a strange land," but also of all the other places where the Bible uses the theme of exile, of dispossession, of wandering in the wilderness. Jesus seems quite deliberately to adopt this motif in his relations to the Temple at Jerusalem. The Son of Man has "nowhere to lay his head." He makes his friends among the despised "people of the land," whose ancestors, ironically, had been excluded from participation in rebuilding the second Temple by the returning Babylonian exiles! These "people of the land" indeed represented the invasion of sacred territory by interlopers who intermarried with the Hebrew dregs left behind at the time of the Exile: proving, I suppose, that one cannot use even the diaspora idea in a geographically absolute way!

New Testament theology further alludes to the theme of dispersion in a variety of ways. The treatments of baptism as a new Exodus and the Eucharist as a new Passover certainly suggest it. But the account of the day of Pentecost leaves no doubt. The outpouring of the Spirit on that day, a clear sign of the coming of the messianic age, is vouchsafed to a crowd of diaspora Jews! Special pains are taken to make clear that these are not regular residents of Jerusalem. Presumably, although thousands of them are received into the messianic community, they do not remain indefinitely in the Holy City. Their business done, they scatter to their homes. Thus the Jewish diaspora is already "seeded" with persons who have been baptized into the Christian faith. The existence of these men in the path of the subsequent Christian mission is surely a significant factor in the success of that mission, although on this point the New Testament is wholly silent.

It would seem as if the foundation of the Christian faith

had been providentially ordered in such a way as to make impossible the adoption for long of any "ecclesiastical" home base such as Jerusalem until the faith had firmly anchored itself in Rome, the symbolical capital of the secular world. No doubt we should regard the "fulness of time" as including the ripeness of Jerusalem for the catastrophe of A.D. 70. And this suggests something else. We have long had to battle a pietist reading of the New Testament which sees Christianity as having turned inward, substituting a private cult (the Upper Room) for the temple sacrifices, and personal salvation (justification by faith) for the social and political involvements of first-century Judaism. The New Testament does not merely transform the public history of God's people into some form of private in-groupism but it has not been easy to communicate what it *does* do. Now we see that with the coming of Christ the people of God accept and embrace their diaspora role. They acknowledge their exclusion from the existing centers of ecclesiastical power and adopt their servant mission. The socio-religious structure of Judaism is left behind for a new period of wilderness-wandering, in which the essential reality of the covenant people is maintained without the accustomed, settled forms of life in Palestine. Jesus does not prepare his followers for withdrawal from public concerns. He prepares them only for withdrawal from the religio-political assumptions of an *aion* that is passing away.

Now the distinctive response of the primitive Church to diaspora existence was not simply an impulse to innovate. Nascent Christianity had already adopted a style of life and worship outwardly resembling that of the synagogue. Nor was the point that "Jerusalem" no longer had significance in Christian thought. The real change was that "Jerusalem" could no longer be the tangible mountain of the Lord about which God's people could gather *in patria*. "Jerusalem" was now an eschatological symbol of the ultimate fulfillment, the site of the expected messianic feast. And it was clear that this fulfillment could not take place until the gospel had been preached to the nations, and until *all* men were gathered at Mount Zion. There *could be no home base* until the final fulfillment. Three centuries later the concordat with Constantine led gradually to an illusion that Rome *was* home! But the illusion had a price. It could only be maintained at the cost of forgetting the eschatological tension in which the Church had begun, of forgetting that the true home base was still in ruins, occupied, defiled, and uninhabitable *until* the final revealing and gathering of the children of God. Any home base which the Church might build on diaspora territory was destined to be of passing meaning, and to the extent that any such home base was absolutized, it was sure to become an idol.

The meaning of living in diaspora, then, is not so much a matter of finding structures that appear formally appropriate for such a scattered existence, "unstructured" structures perhaps, as it is a matter of *understanding how* the diaspora congregation is related to God's purposes for the *oikoumene*, the whole inhabited earth. There is only one possible understanding: The way back to Jerusalem is through mission! And the mission we pursue must not treat our present congregations as if somehow, taken together, they determined the guest list for the final banquet! On the contrary, the New Testament suggests that these congregations of ours are but early appearances within human history of the nature of the consummation. But they fail even to be this if they are not constantly pointing away from themselves *toward* that end. The final gathering, we are told, is Christ's own work. And until that final gathering, the end lies in an outward direction from us, not in a movement inward toward our own centers of understanding or organization.

Practical Steps Toward a New Reformation

The key to many of the most successful new departures in church life today lies, not in the adoption of any novel organizational structure, but in a new vision of what the Church is for. Outwardly, the best experiments use largely traditional "forms." The East Harlem Protestant Parish does what the name implies: it uses the "parish" idea. It has "congregations" with ministers and laity. But yet the difference between this "parish" and many in suburbia is immense! The Church of the Savior in Washington, D.C., again employs a traditional "form," but invests it with new life. Other experiments revive the monastic ideal in varying degree, and so on. I believe that we make a mistake in speaking constantly of "new forms of the life of the Church," because this phrase inevitably suggests an emphasis on sheer innovation, which can and does lead us to an unwillingness to use the forms we have. In more than one case, a well-founded awareness that the existing Church has lost meaning has led, not to renewal, but to paralysis. The real point is that we cannot behave as if we were at home in Jerusalem. We are not building or maintaining Temples. This is not the time for preoccupation with ecclesiastical housekeeping. To confuse the work of the Church with "church work" is to presuppose that there *is* a Temple to be kept straight, whereas what counts so far as the final consummation is concerned is our quality of life as citizens of those communities which *do* exist meaningfully now: the communities we share with our fellow men. In a diaspora situation, in short, the *human community has greater eschatological significance than the ecclesiastical community*. It is "the kingdom of the world" which becomes "the kingdom of Our Lord and of his Christ" (Rev. 11:15). Tinkering with our church structures will not change this fact, or really meet it head on. Only a renewal of the minds with which we understand what we do will avail. With this, the necessary changes in the Church will ensue.

It is important to remember that ecclesiastical structures are always both necessary and expendable. We cannot get things done without *some* form of organization, and yet *any* organizational form tends, like the blackboard diagram, to restrict and codify the imagination. The particular ecclesiastical forms we have today tend to obscure what God is really doing in the world; yet new forms may come in time to do the same thing. It is necessary for our awareness of the work of God always to conflict with the churchly status quo, but to do so without iconoclasm. A critique of the present structure of my own church would be easy to draw up. And certainly the same critique would apply to other Protestant bodies as well. But this would be not to the point. The point is to keep an imaginative distance between ourselves and the organization, remembering that although we are not content with it, we cannot do without it.

Considering our diaspora situation, our church membership lists have on them the wrong people. We do not share the gospel with enough of the people who are on the growing edge of the world's work, and we have in our fellowship too many people who find a place in the Church to hide from what God is doing. We present a picture to the world which belies the gospel in which we believe, and it is doubtful that *we*, considering who we are, can do much about this! God has called other men to his service. Somehow our concept of mission must take account of the fact that we may meet God beyond our walls in a more meaningful way than we find him within, and this turns everything topsy-turvy. I do not believe that we must conclude from this that the line between the Church and the world no longer has meaning. But the meaning is certainly no longer clear to *us*. Many writers are asking whether the "gathered congregation" as we know it can continue to be the basic form of the Church. I would put the question differently: how can the gathered congregation come to do its gathering in the right places and in the right way? Perhaps our evangelistic task is not to gather men into our fellowship as it is, but to gather them so that they, like the Gentiles to whom Paul preached, can in time take the Church over! Our problem, in short, is not one of restructuring ourselves but of giving the possibility of fellowship in Christ, with all the potentiality of new life it embodies, to the world!

Such a development would in turn raise serious questions about the form of church life we know as the "denomination." Denominations exist for servicing congregations of the traditional, inward-looking type. They tend to make congregations self-conscious by placing emphasis on their peculiarity over against other congregations, not to speak of the world. Denominations do not easily give congregations away; for without these local, more or less uniform units, the denomination could not exist. Increasingly, as we explore the life of the new human collocations of our time, it is obvious that multiple and competing denominations cannot begin to meet the requirements of Christian mission. But one must also raise the question of whether a single amalgamated body still addicted to a "denominational" point of view could do better. This is not to say that national and regional church bodies are unnecessary. But it is to say that the new humanity which can emerge from the mass of mankind will call for something very different from our present notion of national church organization. Again, one may ask whether the difficulty may not be less with the organization involved than with *us?* Do we as denominations, though we may be seeking union, speak for what God is doing in America?

Clearly, one cannot engineer changes of the sort that

may be needed. To attempt to do so would be to usurp God's right to call whomever he wills into his Church. The most that we can do is to seek to become instruments of that divine will. There may be a way to do this better than we have been doing. My own church, acting together with others, could take steps to throw much more of its resources and of its support into forms of mission unconnected with existing congregations and not primarily aimed at adding new names to the membership rolls. Already this kind of thing is being done in the inner city, on college campuses, and in a host of other places. At present, however, the structure of my church, with its almost exclusive emphasis on the ministry in its traditional parish form, does not encourage mission which simply gives the church away to the world. If the endless lists of congregational statistics in the minutes of the General Assembly are a guide to the ethos of the denomination, what I am proposing will not quickly win widespread support. But the United Presbyterian Church is, in fact, much more open to non-parochial, and even non-ecclesiastical, ministries than its constitution might suggest. Officially, however, a man who exercises his ministry outside of the denominational or interdenominational ecclesiastical structure, to become an employee, for example, of a university, a factory, a hospital, is in a most anomalous position.

I am suggesting that what we must do is send more and more men outside the structure. We must recognize the existing Church for what it is: a symbolic continuation of the old home base, functioning toward the rest of mankind much as nineteenth-century Europe and America functioned toward the lands to which missionaries were sent. There is no use trying to extend the structure of the home base to the lands of mission. Like the vanished bastion of "Christendom," the home base represented by our existing churches is perishing. It is perhaps allowed by Providence to remain long enough for a probe to be launched out into the new world. The gospel must be allowed to become indigenous in the midst of the new humanity all about us. It is from there that fresh insights may return, as they have from Asia and Africa, to rejuvenate the "older churches" left behind.

I can imagine a re-formed missionary enterprise, conceived along these lines, having immense appeal to the younger generation of ministers and to many laymen in my own denomination. Clearly, such a venture should learn all the lessons the "foreign missionary" enterprise had to teach. It could not be done on other than an interdenominational basis. Whatever forms of church life resulted should be united from the start. Just as the impetus to union today is strongest in Africa and Asia, so denominations in America might have much to learn from the products of their mission at home. But above all, it should be clear that the new Church resulting from such an effort should belong, not to the sponsoring denominations, but to the new men of God's new world. Whether we who are Christians today will have any part in that is for Our Lord to decide.

Daniel J. O'Hanlon, S.J.:

Epilogue

As recently as five years ago, perhaps even three or four, it would have been unusual for a Roman Catholic to be invited to write the conclusion to a book like this. Today it seems almost normal. That change is a measure of the new climate in Protestant-Catholic relations in this country. Climate, I say, for it is not yet clear how much else has been achieved. Yet for this new atmosphere we must be very grateful, since it holds rich promise for the future. It is most appropriate that such an exchange should appear under the auspices of an Anglican editor and publisher. After all, in the movement toward Christian unity, the Anglican communion has acted as a bridge from the beginning. I want to express my warm thanks to Professor William J. Wolf for his generous invitation to contribute to this symposium. I am grateful for the courtesy he has extended to me personally, but even more grateful for the larger significance of this open gesture. It is another sign of spring after a long and dreary winter. Since I have never met even one of the six authors of the preceding essays, I come to the task of commenting on their remarks with considerable reluctance and hesitation. I know I shall fail to understand much of what they have said, and I fear that not all of what I say may be understood. Nevertheless, continuing conversation between Protestants and Catholics is too important for the renewal of all the Churches to be postponed until it can be carried on in ideal circumstances. So enough of these misgivings. Down to business!

The simplest way of handling my assignment seems to be to comment briefly on each of the six essays in turn, and then conclude with some over-all reflections.

Dr. Kitagawa (Anglican) seems to be saying that the principal spur to reformation of all the Churches is the rediscovery of the world. Indeed, for him this discovery appears to be more than a stimulus to self-examination and reform. It is the providential means which both compels the Churches to reform and dictates the patterns of their reformation. Historians of theology will recognize that the plea for accepting the integrity of the secular is not something entirely new. The theological innovation of Aquinas was basically nothing different. His system was bitterly attacked in his day as a betrayal of the all but exclusively supernaturalist Augustinianism, which had prevailed for centuries in Western Christendom. Aquinas insisted that the world has a nature and structure of its own independently of the higher destiny into which it is caught up by Christ's work of redemption. This friendliness of Aquinas to "the world," which earned him the opposition of most of the theologians of his time, is probably much the same thing as the Anglican tradition of incarnational and sacramental theology to which Dr. Kitagawa refers.

Such a theology, if it is really acted on consistently, is a healthy counterbalance to a too exclusively "spiritual" kind of Christianity. I suspect it was a similar concern which lay behind Luther's protest against late-medieval monasticism. He wanted the Gospel to permeate every vocation "in the world." But there seems to be another trend operative in Protestantism since the time of the Reformation. In reaction against Roman "materialism" and "hierarchical institutional-ism" there has been a strong suspicion of any Christianity which is not purely spiritual. Perhaps what Dr. Kitagawa is asking is that the Reformation plea for the Gospel in the world be given more attention today than the other principle which insists too much and in the wrong places on a purely "spiritual" Christianity.

I heartily share his desire to make Christians responsible for building a society in which men can lead a truly human life. I admire his willingness to modify the pastoral structures of the Church to suit the new sociological patterns of an automated, urbanized, open, world-wide society in which Christians are—perhaps forever—a minority. I agree that the Church should see its mission to the world as one of service and not of domination.

However, at one point I have some misgivings. Surely the Christian message is something more than a ratification of the secular, more than a mere discovery of the meaning which already lies hidden in the secular. Has not the redemptive work of Christ given a really new dimension to human history?

Dr. Leavenworth's essay (Baptist) points in a different direction. Instead of concentrating his attention on the world and conceiving reform primarily as a response triggered by the challenge of the world, he has turned his attention inward in a very humble and searching ecclesiastical examination of conscience. I found more genuine concern for serious and specific internal reform of the Church in this essay than in any of the other five. To read Dr. Leavenworth's honest and open description of definite areas where Baptists need reform was for me a very moving experience. There is an earnest grappling with the problem of authority in the Church, a desire to recover contact with the corporate witness of the Church across the centuries, a willingness to consider and accept the elements of truth in non-Baptist approaches to Baptism. My impression from Dr. Leavenworth's essay is that the Baptists do indeed have treasures, that there surely is "a pulsing catholicity about the Baptist witness that needs to be articulated," and that the ecumenical movement will profit immensely as Baptist participation increases. If this essay is a reliable indication, then what Baptists have in common with other Christians, at least with Catholics, really is far more significant than their distinctive differences.

Dr. Durgin (United Church) explains and defends three Christian realities: freedom, autonomy of the local church, and the priesthood of all believers. All three of these are extremely important, especially in the current reformation going on within the Roman Catholic Church.* But I looked for a somewhat different emphasis in a symposium of this kind. As I understand the assignment given to the contributors, they were to attempt to outline, from the Protestant side, a program corresponding to the current Catholic effort "to fulfill the justified demands of Lutherans, Calvinists, Orthodox, Anglicans and Free Churchmen in the light of the Gospel of Jesus Christ." In Catholic efforts to meet these justified demands these three themes should and do appear. But from the Protestant side I would have expected more than a reassertion of these characteristically Protestant emphases. Without minimizing freedom, I would have welcomed an examination of how order and authority might find a larger place in the life of the Protestant Churches. Without prejudice to the legitimate autonomy of the local church, it would have been good to see an exploration of how the corporate unity of the

---

* See *Council Speeches of Vatican II* (Glen Rock, N.J.: Deus Books, 1964), edited by Hans Küng and others. Bishop Ernest Primeau, "Responsible Freedom of the Layman," pp. 83-86; Bishop Emile Joseph de Smedt, "The Priesthood of All Believers," pp. 39-43.

Church universal could be strengthened. While retaining, even reaffirming the priesthood of all believers, would it not have been possible to give some attention to the role of the ordained minister and his special function in the Christian community?

My objection is not that freedom, local autonomy, and the priesthood of all believers are irrelevant issues in the reform of the Church. They are highly relevant—for Catholics. But in a Protestant essay in *this* symposium it seems to me that consideration of their counterbalancing correlates would have been more appropriate.

When he speaks of Lutheran seminary reform, Professor Lazareth voices the concern which is steadily growing among Catholics as well. "Theology," he reminds us, "is to be taught, learned, attacked and defended within the universal context of man's total quest for truth in the midst of all the principalities and powers of the university world." Such a change would compel professors and students to relate the Gospel to the contemporary situation and would raise academic standards more effectively than any other single move. It is no accident that today, both in Europe and America, the most influential theology comes out of theological faculties which are affiliated with large universities.

What Dr. Williams seems to deplore in Methodism more than anything else is institutional inertia. This, he feels, prevents Methodists from being free for Christ's work in the world. The emphasis on mission as a principal mark of the Church, the concern for new forms of missionary presence of the Church, especially through lay ministries, echo what was said by Dr. Kitagawa. The essay left me with the same kind of uneasiness I felt after reading Kitagawa's. The Church most certainly has a mission to the world, the whole world, and she belongs out in the midst of change. But she needs a strong life of her own before she can fulfil that mission. She must *be* something if she is to *give* something.

Dr. Williams surely knows the problems of his own Church, and institutional inertia can admittedly be maddening at times. But if this symposium is concerned to examine those reforms in Protestantism which meet the legitimate demands of Catholics, other issues would seem to take precedence over a call for openness to new forms of mission to the world.

Professor Mudge's essay (Presbyterian) begins with great promise. He points to the need of Protestant bodies to reconsider their ecclesiological assumptions and constitutional structures. He goes on to say—rightly, I think—that the new reformation which Küng and others are seeking surely looks to this virtually untouched level of action. However, he soon yields to the apparently overpowering fascination of the current themes: the secular, the metropolis, parish sociology, the diaspora situation of the Church. Most of what Kitagawa and Williams had said is repeated in slightly different form.

Let me make it clear that I consider all these themes to be of tremendous importance. No Church serious about reform can overlook them. One might even say that the measure of successful reform will be the degree to which the Church is able to fulfill its mission to the world. As far as the Catholic Church is concerned, Vatican II has placed this problem as the final one for which the others (self-awareness of the Church, renewal of the Church, Christian unity) are preliminary. The question I am raising is this: when charting those areas of Protestant reform which respond to legitimate Catholic demands, should top priority be given to the issue of the Church's mission to the world?

Despite their real excellence in other ways, it seems to me that all six of the essays (with the possible exception of the Baptist contribution) fail to consider the kind of reforms which Catholics hope to see in the Protestant Churches. I am driven to conclude that their authors either (a) simply do not know what kind of reform Catholics would like to see in the

Protestant Churches or (b) they consider such Catholic desires quite irrelevant. I prefer to think that the first alternative is the true one.

In reading these essays, I have the impression that their authors (the general editor is an obvious exception) have had no extended dialogue with their Catholic brethren. I do not mean to blame them for this situation. It is quite possible that Catholic indifference and reluctance have much to do with it. All I am saying is that there is little or no evidence in these essays that their authors are carrying on a steady dialogue with Catholics. And that is too bad.

This may be because they understood their assignment as one of self-examination within their own Churches to discover what reforms are needed. Certainly no one, least of all a Catholic, could find fault with such a procedure. This is precisely what the Roman Catholic Church is now doing. She has embarked on a program of internal reform.

But I am convinced that no reform of any of the Churches today can be carried on in isolation from the others. Indeed, it is the isolation itself of the Christian Churches from each other which must above all be reformed. Much of the stimulation to internal reform and the identification of specific areas of reform have come to the Roman Catholic Church, and continue to come, from its study of the other Christian Churches and its dialogue with them. Is it unreasonable to expect that Protestants may find similar help from studying the Catholic Church and carrying on dialogue with Catholics?

"Then tell us," you might feel inclined to ask, "what it is that Protestantism can learn from Catholicism? What are the 'justified demands' of Catholics for reform in the other Christian Churches?" My reply, in all honesty, is that there is no other realistic way for Protestants to find this out but to embark on a serious study of the Catholic Church and engage in continuing dialogue with Catholics. It would do no good for me to make out a list of "demands." And it could do harm. Only when Protestants choose to conduct a careful evaluation of contemporary Catholicism in the light of the Gospel will they be able to discover what in conscience they can accept and use in their own programs of internal reform. I think it would be presumptuous for a Catholic to compile a list of "justified Catholic demands," particularly in a short paragraph in a brief epilogue. In these matters, both Protestants and Catholics must make their own discoveries through the long process of personal study and face-to-face discussion.

That is why it saddens me to look in vain for evidence in the foregoing essays that the authors are engaged in continuing dialogue with Catholics. I know that some Protestants carry on such conversations regularly. And it would be unfair to overlook the generous initiative of the editor and publisher in giving this book a Catholic epilogue. For that let me once again express my sincere thanks. But there is still a long road ahead of us. We have hardly begun.

Contributors' Notes

Introduction

1. *New Republic*, May 18, 1963, p. 8.
2. Hans Küng, *The Council in Action* (New York: Sheed & Ward, 1963), pp. 23-4.
3. *Union Quarterly Review*, January, 1964, p. 102.
4. Hans Küng, *op. cit.*, p. 27.
5. *Faith and Order Trends*, December, 1963, p. 7.

1.   Toward an Ecumenical Theology of Mission and Ministry

1. See, among others: Denys Munby, *The Idea of a Secular Society* (New York: Oxford U.P., 1963); Paul Van Buren, *The Secular Meaning of the Gospel* (New York: Macmillan, 1963); John A. T. Robinson, *Honest to God* (Philadelphia: Westminster Press, 1963).
2. Cf. Gibson Winter, *The New Creation as Metropolis* (New York: The Macmillan Co., 1963), esp. Ch. II, "The Servant Church in a Secularized World."

2.   Do the Baptists Have Treasures?

1. Samuel S. Hill, Jr. and Robert G. Torbet, *Baptist North and South* to be published by Judson Press, Valley Forge, Pa., in 1964, p. 12.

2. Norman H. Maring and Winthrop S. Hudson, *A Baptist Manual of Polity and Practice* (Valley Forge: Judson Press, 1963), p. 4.

3. *Ibid.*

4. *Ibid.*, p. 7.

5. Robert G. Torbet, *The Baptist Story* (Valley Forge: Judson Press, 1957), p. 117.

6. Maring and Hudson, *op. cit.*, p. 200.

7. Walter J. Harrelson develops this theme in his chapter "The Biblical Basis of the Gospel," in *Great Themes in Theology*, edited by Lynn Leavenworth (Valley Forge: Judson Press, 1958), Ch. 1, pp. 21 ff. He affirms that "The early creeds and confessions of Baptists demonstrate that the Bible was looked upon as of indubitable authority." He refers to the British H. Wheeler Robinson's book *The Life and Faith of the Baptists* (London: Methuen and Co., Ltd., 1927) and A. H. Newman (Southern Baptist), *A History of the Baptist Churches in the United States* (New York: Charles Scribner's Sons, 1894). "Robinson's constant appeal to Scripture helped to make and keep Baptists a Bible-loving church" (p. 8., Newman). "Baptists . . . are anxious to be instructed in the word of God . . . and are ready to abandon any position that can be shown to be out of harmony with apostolic precept . . ." (p. 7).

8. Harrelson, in L. Leavenworth, ed., *op. cit.*, pp. 28-29.

9. *Ibid.*, p. 44.

10. Fritz Blanke, "Anabaptism and the Reformation," p. 57, in the very fine book of essays edited by Guy F. Hershberger, *The Recovery of the Anabaptist Vision* (Herald Press, 1957). This group of twenty-five essays is a result of Anabaptist-Mennonite research and rediscovery. There is an important library representing the modern upsurge of historiography among the Mennonites (covering modern Anabaptist writings in Europe and America) in the Mennonite Historical Library of Goshen College.

11. Emil Brunner, *Misunderstanding of the Church* (Philadelphia: Westminster Press, 1953).

12. John Knox, *The Church and the Reality of Christ* (New York: Harper & Row, 1962).

13. Albert C. Outler, *The Christian Tradition and the Unity We Seek* (Oxford University Press, 1957), or the World Council studies, such as *The Universal Church in God's Design* (New York: Harper & Brothers, 1948).

14. *Foundations*, Vol. 1, No. 2 (April, 1958), p. 45.

15. *Ibid.*, p. 49.

16. Maring and Hudson, *A Baptist Manual of Polity and Practice*, p. 181.

17. Duke K. McCall (ed.), *What is the Church?*, Ch. IV, p. 64.

18. *Foundations*, Vol. III, No. 1 (January, 1960), p. 74.

19. *Ibid.*, p. 82.

20. A. Gilmore (ed.), *Christian Baptism* (Philadelphia: Judson Press, 1959).

21. *Ibid.*, p. 308.

22. *Ibid.*, p. 309.

23. *Ibid.*, p. 311.

24. *Ibid.*, p. 316.

25. *Ibid.*, p. 317.

26. *Ibid.*, p. 324.

27. *Foundations*, Vol. III, No. 1, p. 6.

28. Michael J. Taylor, *The Protestant Liturgical Renewal* (Westminster, Md.: The Newman Press, 1963).

29. *Ibid.*, p. xvii.

30. *Ibid.*, p. 264.

31. Dr. Taylor lists the various articles on baptism in recent issues of *Foundations*, the British book on *Christian Baptism* which we have discussed.

32. *The Protestant Liturgical Renewal*, p. 268.

33. *Ibid.*, pp. 272-273.

3. *Christ Has Set Us Free*

1. William Stringfellow, *Free in Obedience* (New York: The Seabury Press, 1964), pp. 50-51.

2. Paul Tillich, *The Courage to Be* (Yale University Press, 1959), p. 190.

3. P. T. Forsyth, *The Principle of Authority* (London: Independent Press, 1952), p. 281.

4. Paul Tillich, *Systematic Theology*, III (The University of Chicago Press, 1963), p. 239.

5. P. T. Forsyth, *The Church and the Sacraments* (London: Independent Press, 1955), pp. 68-69.

6. J. S. Whale, *The Protestant Tradition* (Cambridge University Press, 1955), p. 342.

7. Hans Küng, *The Council in Action* (New York: Sheed & Ward, 1963), p. 236.

8. *Ibid.*, p. 236.

9. Yngve Brilioth, *Eucharistic Faith and Practice Evangelical and Catholic* (London: S.P.C.K., 1961), p. 274.

10. P. T. Forsyth, *The Church and the Sacraments* (London: Independent Press, 1955), p. 272.

11. Hans Küng, *op. cit.*, p. 119.

12. From the hymn "O God of Earth and Altar," text by Gilbert K. Chesterton, from a traditional Welsh melody.

13. Paul Tillich, *Systematic Theology*, III, p. 245.

4. *The Future of American Lutheranism*

1. Wilhelm Pauck, *The Heritage of the Reformation* (Glencoe, Ill.: Free Press, 1961), p. 102.

2. Luther D. Reed, *The Lutheran Liturgy* (Philadelphia: Muhlenberg Press, 1947), p. 225.

3. Theodore G. Tappert (ed.), *The Book of Concord* (Philadelphia: Muhlenberg Press, 1959), p. 59.

4. Conrad Bergendoff, "The Meaning of Lutheran Unity," *The Lutheran Companion*, Nov. 5, 1952.

5. *Messages of the Helsinki Assembly* (Minneapolis: Augsburg Publishing House, 1963), pp. 121-122.

6. Conrad Bergendoff, *The Lutheran Church in America and Theological Education* (LCA Board of Theological Education, 1963).

7. *Church and State—A Lutheran Perspective* (LCA Board of Social Ministry, 1963), p. 33.

8. Winthrop Hudson, *American Protestantism* (University of Chicago Press, 1961), p. 176.

5.   On Being Free for Christ's Work in the World

1. *The Journal of John Wesley*, II (standard ed.; London: The Epworth Press, 1938), pp. 168-172.

2. John Wesley, *Works*, VIII, pp. 322-324.

6.   Can Presbyterians Be Reformed?

1. See, for example, Gibson Winter, *The New Creation as Metropolis* (New York: Macmillan, 1963), pp. 38 ff.

2. "The Form of the Church in the Modern Diaspora," *The Princeton Seminary Bulletin*, Vol. LVII, No. 3 (March, 1964), pp. 3-18.

The Contributors

WILLIAM J. WOLF, TH.D., S.T.D., is Howard Chandler Robbins Professor of Theology at the Episcopal Theological School, Cambridge, Massachusetts. Dr. Wolf was an official observer at both sessions of Vatican Council II.

LAWRENCE L. DURGIN, D.D., is Pastor of the Broadway Congregational Church, United Church of Christ; President of the Manhattan Division of the Protestant Council; member of the Advisory Committee of the Department of Faith and Order Studies of the National Council of Churches.

DAISUKE KITAGAWA, D.D., is an executive secretary in the Home Department of the National Council of the Protestant Episcopal Church.

WILLIAM H. LAZARETH, PH.D., presently Professor of Systematic Theology at the Philadelphia Lutheran Seminary, represents the Lutheran Church in America on the Faith and Order Commission of the World Council of Churches.

J. LYNN LEAVENWORTH, B.D., PH.D., has been Director of Department of Theological Education, American Baptist Convention, since 1951; editor of *Great Themes in Theology*.

LEWIS S. MUDGE, PH.D., is Associate Professor of Religion and Philosophy, and Minister to Amherst College, Amherst, Massachusetts; member of the Advisory Committee on Faith and Order, NCC; Secretary of the Department of Theology of the World Presbyterian Alliance from 1957 to 1962.

DANIEL J. O'HANLON, S.J., is Professor of Fundamental Theology, Alma College, California Jesuit School of Theology; visiting Professor of Religion at Stanford University, California.

COLIN W. WILLIAMS, B.D., PH.D., formerly Professor of Systematic Theology at Queens College, University of Melbourne, is at present Executive Director of the Central Department of Evangelism of the National Council of the Churches of Christ in the U.S.A. and Chairman of the Department on Studies in Evangelism of the World Council of Churches.

Date Due